BEYOND
SCHOOL IMPROVEMENT

BEYOND
SCHOOL IMPROVEMENT

The Journey
to Innovative Leadership

Robert Davidovich

Pauli Nikolay • Bonnie Laugerman • Carol Commodore

Foreword by Rick Stiggins

CORWIN
A SAGE Company

For information:

Corwin
A SAGE Company
2455 Teller Road
Thousand Oaks, California 91320
(800) 233-9936
Fax: (800) 417-2466
www.corwinpress.com

SAGE Ltd.
1 Oliver's Yard
55 City Road
London EC1Y 1SP
United Kingdom

SAGE Pvt. Ltd.
B 1/I 1 Mohan Cooperative
   Industrial Area
Mathura Road, New Delhi 110 044
India

SAGE Asia-Pacific Pte. Ltd.
33 Pekin Street #02-01
Far East Square
Singapore 048763

Printed in the United States of America

Library of Congress Cataloging-in-Publication Data

Beyond school improvement: the journey to innovative leadership/Robert Davidovich . . . [et al.].
     p. cm.
Includes bibliographical references and index.
ISBN 978-1-4129-7140-9 (pbk.)
   1. School management and organization—United States. 2. Organizational change—Management—United States. 3. Educational leadership—United States. 4. Strategic planning—United States. I. Davidovich, Robert. II. Title.

LB2805.B49 2010
371.2'07—dc22   2009031799

This book is printed on acid-free paper.

09   10   11   12   13   10   9   8   7   6   5   4   3   2   1

Acquisitions Editor:	Arnis Burvikovs
Associate Editor:	Desirée Bartlett
Editorial Assistant:	Joanna Coelho
Production Editor:	Veronica Stapleton
Copy Editor:	Codi Bowman
Typesetter:	C&M Digitals (P) Ltd.
Proofreader:	Jennifer Gritt
Indexer:	Molly Hall
Cover Designer:	Anthony Paular

Contents

Foreword

It is with considerable humility that I introduce you to this volume on innovative school leadership. This is not my field of study; I have to admit to having developed little expertise in these matters. But in this case, my weak background represents an advantage because I, hopefully like you, come to the book with the intent of learning its lessons. And as I studied it, I did learn a great deal.

First, with respect to the nature of the presentation offered and arguments advanced, clearly, these authors are far more than excellent scholars—they are teachers and leaders who have structured the presentation accordingly. The learning aids they have woven into the text direct readers—hopefully working in leadership teams—into activities that both support their mastery of the ideas being presented and their transformations of those ideas into reflections, conversations, and actions that make the authors' ideas come alive in the readers' organizations. For instance, readers are frequently asked to "take a moment" to reflect on what is being presented and to connect it to their personal professional experience. Each chapter concludes with very thoughtful self-assessments that spur teamwork in the service of systemic school improvement. And all of this is tied together with a variety of practical examples of innovation playing out in real school contexts.

Next, with respect to the content of this presentation, again, I do not feel qualified to comment on innovative leadership. But I can address the relevance of the authors' position on how we must understand and carry out change in schools. They want us to think of innovation in terms of embracing dissonance, creating context, changing our field of perception, and letting ideas collide. My domain of professional practice is assessment. Nowhere in the development of schools of the future do we need a new vision more than in the area of assessment. As I read this book, it was increasingly clear to me how the process of innovation connects directly to the experience we are living right now in the assessment arena. Let me share several illustrations.

I live my life striving to induce dissonance among practitioners and policymakers alike, by questioning and confronting decades of belief that the path to school improvement is paved with more and better annual standardized multiple-choice tests. Six decades of districtwide, statewide, national, international, and (soon!) interplanetary testing, at a cost of billions over the years with little research evidence of positive impact on school quality, must be confronted. It's not that such testing is inappropriate—it's that it is insufficient. It fails to meet the information needs of the most important instructional decision makers—teachers and students—whose needs can only be served by long-ignored yet critically important day-to-day classroom applications of assessment. Traditional assessment beliefs and practices have run exactly counter to what we know to be sound practices. Are there other domains besides assessment where this might be the case and where we must embrace dissonance to spur action? The authors advise that there are and it is time to confront them. And I agree.

Further, they advise us to "create context" by establishing the relevance of innovation in the minds of the colleagues with whom we work. Create a constituency that shares a vision of sound practice and is willing to advocate for it. Again, nowhere is that more critical these days than in the realm of assessment. Traditional beliefs have held that teachers teach and assessment people gather the data on effectiveness and never the twain shall meet. As a result, it remains the case, in 2010, that preservice teacher and administrator preparation programs are still devoid of any relevant helpful assessment training. Historically, there has been no constituency built to demand sound assessment practice. But professional development opportunities to learn are becoming more plentiful, and we understand how to fill those opportunities with the key lessons that teachers and school leaders need to master to fulfill their rapidly evolving assessment responsibilities. Without question, future schools will be filled with practitioners who understand how to transform the traditional testing culture to a learning culture where assessment is a learning tool. Are there other school context realities that need a push in this direction? Again, the authors say yes, there are, and I concur.

The presentation offered herein advocates for the long view of school quality—for a distant look toward what schools can become—for a new field of view and vision. It urges local leadership teams to unshackle from the view of the past and entertain the possibility that schools and classrooms might need to evolve to respond to the evolution of our society. In my assessment realm, this screams for a view of assessment that takes it far beyond merely serving as an accountability tool—as a source of intimidation for teachers and their students. Imagine a world where an entire generation of students view assessment as a tool that helped them gain the confidence they needed to gain mastery over something that they believed would have otherwise been beyond their reach—something they had been hesitant to strive for. Imagine those students watching themselves succeed and, thus, feeling in complete control of their success as it unfolds. Imagine assessment as something, therefore, that they look forward to. All of this is achievable in classrooms today if we take the risk of aspiring to it. Are there other dimensions of the schooling processes besides assessment that might need this kind of new field of view? I think there are.

Finally, the authors encourage us to let ideas collide. In their big picture, they want us to embrace (indeed, create) dissonance, build learning communities to confront it, bring new ideas to the mix, and let those ideas fight with one another to discover the synergy among them or the superiority of some over others. Nowhere has the competition of visions played out more compellingly than in the domain of assessment practice: norm-referenced versus criterion-referenced interpretation of results, classroom versus large-scale assessment, formative versus summative assessment, assessment *of* learning versus assessment *for* learning, selected versus constructed response. Over the past two decades, these competitions have begun to resolve themselves in research conducted around the world. The results are guiding us toward a deep rethinking of assessment's role in the development of effective schools. Classroom assessments used in support of student learning (assessment *for* learning—a formative application) have emerged as most promising. Are there other dimensions of classroom practice that might be clarified for us in this manner if we permit other *idea collisions* like this one? The authors believe there are—and so do I.

Organizational change, the authors tell us, requires the development of productive risk-taking attitudes and values within those practitioners who would lead the organization into a more productive future. They must figure out where we are now, where we want to be, and then act purposefully to close the gap. This volume provides a path to school innovation in just these terms. The authors have given me a new way to look at my work, and I believe they will do the same for you.

Rick Stiggins, PhD
Assessment Training Institute
Portland, Oregon

Preface

If your actions inspire others to dream more, learn more, do more, and become more, you are a leader.

—John Quincy Adams

The world our students are growing up in, and will inherit, is changing at an almost incomprehensible speed. What these future adults will do as work and play may not even be in our imaginations yet. Thus, as educators, we need to develop schools and learning opportunities that prepare our students to be successful in an unpredictable global world. This requires leaders to not only lead in ways that help our schools get better but also in ways that help them become different. Many authors in the field of education are writing about how to improve teaching and learning, but our premise is that improvement is not enough; classrooms and schools need to innovate at the same time they improve. This creates a challenge for leaders—to help their school organizations improve at the same time they help them innovate.

The point of this book is to start conversations about what it means to lead for improvement *and* innovation. Whether your district is small or large, urban or rural, rich or poor or the facilities are new or old, the challenges and obstacles are the same: using the tension between where you want to be and where you are as a creative force to become different, as well as better. This challenge involves knowing when to enhance current capacities and when to seek solutions that are beyond your school's current capacities. This second aspect, knowing not only when but also how to seek solutions outside of current capacities, involves adding new skills to your leadership repertoire.

In this book, we hope to change your mind-set about what is possible for schools and about what it takes to lead into the future. We hope to scratch an itch you never knew you had or the one that's been nagging you forever. We hope to stimulate courageous conversations within you and to take you to deeper levels of thought and to higher levels of action.

Who are *we?* you might be asking yourself as you read this Preface. Well, we are four friends who have shared experiences and have grown close over the years. We each have more than 30 years of experience as educational leaders. Collectively, we have been teachers, principals, central office administrators, and served at our state's department of public instruction. Additionally, we have taught at the university level and have served as consultants. Our friendship is an oasis where our learning thirst is quenched, challenged, and forever evolving. Perhaps more important, our friendship is a place where we challenge one another to think more deeply, more holistically, more connectedly than we can anywhere else.

Our work together mirrors the process of innovation we discuss in this book. The ideas we wrestled with not only informed our thinking; they formed us. As ideas emerged, we discussed, debated, and dialogued. All the while, these ideas were evolving our thinking and changing how we saw the world and where we fit in it—the ideas formed us. Our working sessions were truly a learning laboratory. We never knew when one small comment would trigger a seismic response that reordered our thoughts in a more potent and powerful way.

This kind of learning is genuine and adaptive because it is a dynamic process where new ideas and past practice interact, and new context is created. It is learning where ideas evolve into deep meaning. In this kind of learning, ideas evolve because they collide with other ideas.

This collision of ideas is often messy, and it can make participants feel uncomfortable. Yet this business of messes and collisions is the only way individuals and systems transform. We have begun to see that educational systems are truly facing a dilemma. To address the future, innovation is an absolute must for our current system of education. Yet our current leaders have been acculturated to improve the current system. Improving and innovating are very different and require completely different skill sets for success.

In our work, we have begun to integrate practices based on this understanding. As we talk to others about our ideas, we usually get an interesting reaction. It is almost as if we observe an awakening. The ideas we have shared create a spark in those we talk with. It is as if the principles we discuss are present yet dormant within them. The message seems to strike a chord, and the timing seems right—thus, this book.

In this book, we offer you a similar inner journey intended to help you transform the way you lead. Being on a journey means that you, as the reader, need to make meaning of the new ideas you will be experiencing along the way. So we have expectations for you:

1. You can't change your system until you change yourself. Get to know yourself better. The book is about linking you to yourself, creating the energy to move beyond where you are now, and finding the courage to transform.

2. Be patient and reflective with yourself. Be involved with honest, deep, reflective thought, and learn to have courageous conversations with yourself. Trust the "becoming" nature of the journey: who you are now and the you that is becoming a more potent leader.

3. Reflect on how the concepts make sense to you in your situation. Always reference new ideas to your situation and your actions.

4. Use the Glossary (Resource A) at the end of book to help you refer to terms as you read the book and do the activities.

5. Engage in all of the *Take a Moment* reflections and other activities so that you can honestly gauge your progress as you move through the book.

6. Follow your development with the Continuum of Leadership Behavior for Creating Change. Your growth will be a pleasant surprise for you.

Finally, we hope that, as you read, you feel a renewed optimism about the future of education and that you develop an enhanced capacity to make a difference in the lives you touch. You have our best wishes and deepest admiration as you embark on the journey to more potent leadership as a teacher, principal, superintendent, board member, or professor.

Acknowledgments

It is with humility, gratitude, and deep appreciation that we thank the people who gave us their support and encouragement during the development of this book. It is because of their ongoing words of confidence and gentle nudging that what was once a faint dream has become a reality.

Most significant, we want to acknowledge our spouses Gerda, Ron, George, and Jim whose support is constant and immeasurable. Additionally, our children and grandchildren, our angels both big and small, motivated our work, for it is they, and their peers, who will most benefit from having passionate leaders who will inspire them to become the leaders of tomorrow. We are humbled as we thank our parents, always in our hearts, who everyday teach us the value of life, love, family, and dreams.

We owe a special debt of gratitude to our friends and colleagues in the College of Education and Leadership at Cardinal Stritch University who have influenced our thinking, disturbed our perceptions, and expanded our vision. They planted the seed and pushed us to higher levels of engagement in the development of this book.

Corwin gratefully acknowledges the contributions of the following individuals:

John W. Adamus, Assistant Professor
Graduate School of Education, Rutgers University
New Brunswick, NJ

Randel Beaver, Superintendent
Archer City ISD
Archer City, TX

Marie Blum, Superintendent
Canaseraga Central School District
Canaseraga, NY

Sister Camille Anne Campbell, Principal
Mount Carmel Academy
New Orleans, LA

Ned Cooper, Leadership Coach and Instructor
Baker College, Central Michigan University
Ann Arbor, MI

Caitilin Dewey, Curriculum Coordinator
Greater Southern Tier Boards of Cooperative Educational Services
Canaseraga Central School District
Canaseraga, NY

Ann L. Ellis, Associate Professor of Teacher Education
Weber State University
Ogden, UT

Sheila Gragg, Assistant Director of Academics
Ashbury College
Nepean, Ontario, Canada

Douglas Gordon Hesbol, Superintendent
Laraway Community Consolidated School District 70-C
Joliet, IL

Neil MacNeill, Principal
Ellenbrook Primary School
Ellenbrook, WA, Australia

Gayle Wahlin, Director of Leadership Services
DuPage County Regional Office of Education
Wheaton, IL

About the Authors

Dr. Robert Davidovich is a consultant specializing in leadership, transformational change, innovation, systems thinking, and organizational planning. An educator for more than 30 years, he has served students as a teacher, principal, staff development coordinator, and director of organizational development. For 14 years, he was the principal of a U.S. Department of Education School of Excellence. In his role as the director of organizational development, he oversaw the district's transformational planning initiative. Robert is an adjunct instructor and lecturer at local universities and a consultant for organizations in several states regarding system improvement, innovative leadership, and organizational development.

Dr. Pauli Nikolay has served as a teacher, principal, director of instruction, superintendent, and an assistant state superintendent at the Department of Public Instruction. In addition to her consultant work in the area of academic standards and instructional strategies, she facilitates workshops on leadership, culture, and improvement/innovation strategies. She received her state's Association for Supervision and Curriculum Development Educator of the Year Award, the Educational Media Association Administrator of the Year Award, the State Reading Association Outstanding Administrator Award, and the Women's Leader in Education Award. She currently serves as a site coordinator, instructor, and mentor for students in the Master's in Educational Leadership program at Cardinal Stritch University.

Dr. Bonnie Laugerman is a high school principal in a large suburban school district that is listed in *US Newsweek* as one of the top 1,500 high schools in the nation and Number 1 rated high school in sports in the state by *Sports Illustrated*. She is currently leading her district through a process of responding to the needs of the 21st-century learner. She has been an educator for more than 30 years, working in urban and suburban school districts in building and central office leadership capacity. Bonnie is a consultant and adjunct professor for a local university and teaches courses related to brain compatible learning, assessment, curriculum, and teacher supervision and evaluation. She has a special interest in the experience of high school principals shaping a learning culture in their schools.

Dr. Carol Commodore is an independent consultant whose special interests center on leadership, assessment, motivation, and learning. An educator for more than 30 years, she served as a classroom teacher, a department chair, an assistant superintendent, and an assessment coordinator. During her tenure as a district leader, she facilitated the establishment of new programs in the areas of foreign language and balanced assessment. Carol has coauthored two other books in the areas of assessment and leadership. Carol presents and consults for local, state, national, and international organizations across North America, Asia, and the Middle East.

Part I

Leading Beyond Improvement

No one has to be told that the world is moving and changing at an incredible rate. Each of us awakes every morning and feels it in the pace of our lives. Caught up in processing all that we encounter in a day dominates our being—and, over time, it can narrow our focus. What a difference it makes to how we lead our lives when we understand the deeper patterns and trends unfolding around us. It is not often enough that we take the time to reflect and examine these trends and how they shape our lives.

The first part of this book is designed to give educators the opportunity to raise their heads from the diligent, intense efforts of their work to improve student learning to cast a gaze to the horizon. On the horizon is the future. As we focus on the here and now for our students, it is critical that we begin to visualize the future we are headed toward to discern the patterns and trends it presents and what they mean for our students and for our system of education.

Looking to the future we find that the precise definition of what students need to learn, so that they can be prepared for success, is a shifting, moving target—one changing as the dynamics of the world change. Leading in such an environment will require different attributes from leaders than those developed in a time when leadership was based on providing stability, predictability, and control. Throughout this book, we view board members, superintendents, central office personal, principals, teachers, and college/university professors all as educational leaders. Educational leaders will need to learn how to lead in ways that help their systems be responsive and adaptive to the changes in the external environment—to help their systems and the people in them to be courageous and innovative. When we use the term *system* in this book, we are referring to interrelated, independent entities that form a complex, unified whole—both in nature and in social structures.

A leadership mind-set focused only on improving performance will not be enough to help our schools remain vital in the future that awaits them on the horizon. Improving schools is important but not sufficient in this age where what we are preparing students for is rapidly changing. This requires that our systems innovate as well as improve.

In Part I, we share some trends and observations about the future and their potential impact on the system of education. Additionally, we compare and contrast leadership practices that advance improvement to those who foster innovation. Four attributes of innovative systems are presented. An examination of the place for these attributes in traditional organizations is offered. Further analysis of what is required of leaders as they lead for innovation is presented.

As educators, together we face a great challenge. These times call for our systems to become different, as well as better, and we feel a sense of urgency in creating these changes. To prepare for that, we want to change the way you think as a leader—with the ultimate expectation that new thinking changes your leadership behavior.

This book is designed to encourage you, the reader, to stretch your capacity. We encourage you to commit to using the reflective elements we offer in the book. Each chapter provides Take a Moment breaks that give you an opportunity to process information and reflect on its meaning to you and your work. Use them. At the end of each chapter, we provide self-assessment activities. Completing these activities will help you assess your learning and growth. We also provide Team Conversation Starters for those of you who are using this book with a team or study group. Taking the time to complete these activities will greatly enhance your learning and, hopefully, your commitment to leading with a renewed perspective and sense of enlightened hope for yourself and your organization.

Schools in a Changing World   1

Major barriers to successful planning are fear of change, ignorance, uncertainty about the future, and lack of imagination.

—John Maxwell, leadership expert

Men will not believe what does not fit in with their plans or suit their prearrangements.

—Barbara Tuchman, historian

Public schools are our nation's most vital piece of infrastructure—as important as any bridge, road, electrical grid, or subway line to making our economy and our nation work and thrive.

—Randi Weingarten, President
American Federation of Teachers

IN THIS CHAPTER

"No man is an island, entire of itself, every man is a piece of the continent, a part of the main" (Donne, 1623, ¶ 2). John Donne's classic wisdom is intended to help us remember that no one is a self-contained entity. It is also true for organizations: No organization is an island, entire of itself. Every organization is embedded in, and in relationship with, its external environment. For organizations to be healthy in today's world, it is imperative that leaders account for the context in which their organization operates.

In this chapter, we will highlight some of the dynamic changes that are occurring in the larger external environment that will impact your school organization. Our point is not to create a comprehensive, all-inclusive list that you and your organization can use to check off the ones for which

3

you can account. The purpose in sharing some observations about world trends is to disturb your comfort level, just a bit. The idea is to make you curious about the possibilities that could come from dynamic changes in the world, which could impact the learning of students in your school. We believe that leaders are more likely to create the synergy to foster innovations once they are open to moving into the dissonance that surrounds them, trusting that something new and better is part of the journey that lies ahead of them.

Rather than list the things you need to do to be successful in the future, more important, we hope to instill in you the mind-set that change is an opportunity for reframing and reordering, for being adaptive and becoming in sync with the dynamics of the world where your students will live and work. In fact, being a bit unsettled is the only way to start the process where old ideas are released so that new ones can form, "It is when we 'have to get out of the potholes of life' that we change" (Maxwell, 2003, p. 50). This type of change brings opportunity for enlightenment, learning, responding to challenges, and creating new meaning. The relevance of that meaning is something that develops from deep within you and the unique interactions you have with of the people in your organization.

THE NEED FOR IMPROVEMENT

Education has always been, and always will be, future oriented. Whether Stone Age youth learning to hunt from elders or today's first grader learning to read— from ancient times to today— the purpose of education is to prepare students for the future by teaching the knowledge, skills, and attributes necessary for leading a successful life. The benefit is the betterment of the individual as well as the preservation of society— that is why schools exist. Societies expect a lot from their schools, as they should. "Our community vibrancy, personal quality of life, economic viability, and business competitiveness depend on a well-prepared citizenry and workforce. Public education provides the bedrock from which our nation and individual prosperity rise together" (Partnership for 21st Century Skills, 2002, p. 2).

Providing the bedrock for prosperity was a lot easier for schools when societies reflected universal values, when graduating students settled down and worked in the region, and when the overall pace of change was measured in years, not months or days. Being the bedrock of the nation is a lot tougher when societal norms are shifting, trends have global influence, and technology accelerates change to a constant whir. The pace of advancement today means that the responses to change that schools are dealing with are no longer about large-scale responses phased in and implemented over years but about continuous adjustment and timely adaptation to shifts in the external environment.

In the early 1990s, Bob worked in a school district that spent a year carefully planning a new technology curriculum. Then, they turned to diligently implementing it, but as Bob humorously recalls, "We had a tough time implementing it because, as we did, this thing called the Internet kept getting in the way." This is just one example of how significant shifts in the external environment that influence the relevance of teaching and learning can, and do, happen at a different speed than a school organization's response speed.

Societal Shifts

Being responsive to societal shifts is not only a concern for the American system of education, but also it is a widespread concern of systems around the world. Economic development has become the common denominator across global societies. Economic growth depends on societies composed of large numbers of well-educated and trained people. So it is natural for people to turn to their education systems for a well-educated workforce. Yet what it means to be well educated and well trained is a moving target, as new technologies influence business and industry before responses can be developed to the previous trend.

China, India, and countries all throughout Asia are experiencing rapid expansions of their economies. In these countries, schools are expected to produce large numbers of highly trained, educated, and motivated workers capable of working in fields that drive economic expansion, such as engineering and science. The educational systems of these countries have been retooled over the last 50 years to feed the needs of societies rising from third-world status to world economic leaders.

In Europe and the United States, schools are expected to produce students with the skills that complement an already highly trained workforce. Business and industry expect workers to enter their organizations without having to be retrained or reeducated with foundational skills. Additionally, schools in these countries were designed with a close link to broad-based societal needs for a well-educated citizenry. One of the difficulties for these systems is that they reached prominence in the Industrial Age and were designed to meet the societal needs of that time.

> The link of societal well-being and schools is inescapable.

The American system of education was developed as a jewel of the Industrial Age. What was required of workers for most of the 1900s is far different from what is required of workers today. The American system of education was forged on compliance and designed to produce students capable of doing routine work. Then, workers who did what they were told to do were valuable. Today, employers value workers who anticipate needs and make decisions that allow the company to stand out from the crowd while pleasing the customer—people who see new possibilities and act on those for the betterment of the company. The link of societal well-being and schools is inescapable. When things are stable in society, schools are expected to support that stability. And when there are troubles in society, or shifts in norms, schools are relied on to fix things and make adjustments.

Throughout the world, schools are under intense pressure to improve performance and adjust their curriculum in response to shifting demands. Today, societies around the globe are modernizing and transforming—and education is seen as the foundation of progress. It has always been this way, yet today societies are more interconnected and the pace of change is greatly accelerated, putting a great deal of pressure on educational systems to not only keep pace with change but also to lead the way.

The American System of Education

In the United States, school reform with the goal of improving student achievement is a top concern in every school district and in every school building, and for a good reason. As we move into a future where knowledge and its application is the driving force in the world, it is vital that we ensure that all children are well educated. Improving our schools to ensure that all students are successful is an imperative faced by every educator, parent, community member, and civic leader as well as by the students themselves.

For many years, the American system of education was among the best in the world at providing the bedrock for societal prosperity. From varied backgrounds, the American system produced a well-prepared citizenry and a strong workforce. Over the last 50 years, the American citizenry has become more diverse and the expectations of the workforce have changed as society has moved from the Industrial Age through the Information Age and into the Conceptual Age (Pink, 2005). Changes with which the American system of education has struggled to keep pace.

That struggle has created an ongoing national dialogue about the effectiveness of America's schools. The dialogue began in earnest when President Reagan's National Commission on Excellence in Education published its report, *A Nation at Risk* in 1983. Since then, there has been an ever-increasing perception that public schools are failing—failing to educate students and prepare them for success in the world of work.

The shock waves of that report left educators scrambling—to this day—to improve the education system. Responses to the claims of failing schools led to the effective schools movement of the 1980s, the standards-based education reform movement of the 1990s and The No Child Left Behind Act (NCLB) of 2001. A quarter century of reform movements and initiatives have improved the nation's schools to some extent, yet they have not erased the perception that they are not adequately preparing students for the future.

In the United States, every educator feels the pressure of accountability to improve a system whose ability to prepare students for the future has been challenged. The comments of former United States Secretary of Education Margaret Spellings (2008) reflect the world most American educators live in: "Test scores are up. The achievement gap is narrowing. According to the Nation's Report Card, since 2000, more kids are learning reading and math. In math especially, we're making great progress. And the children once left behind are making some of the greatest gains" (Spellings, 2008). Hope for a brighter future rises in educators when they consider data such as this. Yet the former Secretary also points out that while improvements are being made there is still much cause for concern:

> Half the black and Hispanic kids who walk into a school do not walk out with a diploma. . . . Scores on the SAT and ACT are flat. Only 42 percent are really ready for college work. . . . In 1975, America was number one in college completion rates. In 2005, we were number 10. And the world continues to pass us by. (Spellings, lines 35–36, 97–98, 66–68)

As the national debate about the effectiveness of schools rages on, statistics can be generated that support a case for failing schools, and they can also be generated to support a case that the education system is getting better. Numbers aside, the bottom line is that every educator is aware of a pervasive belief that the American system is not meeting the learning needs of many students. There is a sense that too

> It is no surprise that improvement and accountability dominate our educational agendas.

many students are not being adequately educated: thus the 2001 federal legislation to *leave no child behind.* Additionally, even for those who are not left behind, businesses complain that high school and college graduates do not possess the skills and dispositions necessary for success in the workforce. It is no surprise that improvement and accountability dominate our educational agendas.

ARE OUR SCHOOLS BROKEN?

The underlying mind-set of the national improvement agenda appears that our schools are broken and in need of repair. It is easy to fall into a mind-set that sees it this way. Seeing it as broken and needing to be fixed means that one views the system of education as if it were a machine.

A Mechanistic Mind-Set

As a society that gained prominence in the Industrial Age, it is only natural to think of the systems around us in mechanistic terms. With a mechanistic mind-set, the common approach to fix something is to replace a faulty part to get the system up and running again. In institutions and organizations, this translates into replacing policies and practices with new ones. Often, these changes come from outside legislation or the top of the organization in the form of mandates that define improvement initiatives. The belief is that by setting performance expectations and regulations that hold schools accountable to those expectations, the system of education will be brought back under control. It is widely believed that then—and only then—the system will produce expected outcomes.

Although there are benefits to improvement initiatives derived from this mind-set, there are also downsides. At the top of the downsides list is the way leaders are acculturated to deal with change. The idea is to get back on track as quickly as possible. Leaders are expected to take corrective measures to fix what is broken or not up to standard. Improvement comes from measured performance and feedback that regulates the outputs of the system to achieve effectiveness. To assess effectiveness, it is necessary to measure performance over time. In doing so, improvement tends to become incremental—occurring in measured steps. In this mind-set, the tendency is for people to seek solutions from current understanding and to focus on the present—taking their view away from the future.

Many educational leaders feel an additional pressure. When they consider the world the students are moving into and how rapidly it is changing, they feel pressure not only to improve their systems but also to make them more relevant. They inherently understand that the Industrial Age assets of compliance and conformity are not good matches for the Conceptual Age.

In the Conceptual Age, successful workers will be those who understand and interpret "the connections between diverse and seemingly separate disciplines" (Pink, 2005, p. 130). As Pink says, they must, "become adept at analogy—at seeing one thing in terms of another" (p. 130). In short, these leaders understand that future success means developing different kinds of attributes in students than is currently achieved. This often causes leaders to feel trapped; they feel pressure to improve this year's test scores and work diligently to do so. Yet they also feel they should be preparing students for the future—to do this they need to expand the view of what and how kids are learning.

A Living System Mind-Set

With a focus narrowly fixed on this year's test performance, it is difficult for leaders to shift their organization's attention to what is occurring on the horizon. The intense pressure of accountability to improvement makes it easy to see why so many leaders stick to addressing immediate concerns and avoid broader attempts to help their systems adjust to the context of a changing future. Doing so involves lifting heads up from the present to consider what the future may bring. Often the future seems too distant to matter, as if it were a mirage on the horizon. To shift focus from the present may take attention away from increasing this year's scores—a risky thing to do for leaders who are intent on analyzing performance and fixing the parts.

As consultants, we find that the leaders we work with are looking for ways to help their systems adapt to changes in the environment, but they just do not know how to break free of the mind-set of incremental improvement. We believe that many educational leaders across the country feel the same—they have a deep desire to lead beyond improving this year's test scores and are looking for new ways of thinking about the leadership needed to get them started. We hope to speak to and nurture these leaders through this book—the ones who feel that improving is not enough, that changing in response to the future is also important.

A quote from Senge, Cambron-McCabe, Lucas, Smith, Dutton, and Kleiner (2000) has greatly influenced our work with school leaders, and we offer it here: "Schools are not 'broken' and in need of fixing. They are a social institution under stress that needs to evolve" (p. 51–52). Machines are something we fix, and our improvements make them better. Living systems make adjustments and adapt to the changes around them to survive. So what would it look like if the national agenda for schools could be aimed toward seeing them as living systems, with the challenge to help them advance in response to a changing world, as opposed to fixing them to make them better?

TAKE A MOMENT

Is your school district tinkering to make the current learning system better and/or is it seeking to redefine the relevance of learning and making changes based on a richer understanding of future needs? How are discussions about the future handled in your school district?

TRENDS IN THE EXTERNAL ENVIRONMENT

To begin the process of helping school systems respond to a changing world, it is important to raise our heads from the important work of improving performance and look to the horizon. Possibilities there shape the context of educators' work—after all, it is where students are headed. To prepare students, educators need to account for the ideas and concepts that will influence their students' future. One way to do that is to look for trends so that leaders can uncover the patterns of change rather than seeing change as series of isolated events. In the following section, several themes will be discussed that represent trends that must be accounted for if school leaders are to help their systems operate synergistically with their environments to prepare students for future success.

- Access to information and the power of the individual
- Accelerating technological advancement
- The changing nature of work and global competition for jobs

Access to Information and the Power of the Individual

Information and power are closely linked. For centuries, those who had information used it to rule over those who did not. Long ago, only the elite had access to information and knowledge, and they kept it from those in lower classes to stand above them. Gutenberg and his printing press changed that, making information accessible to many who previously did not have it. Information has been moving faster and becoming accessible to more and more people ever since. From the telegraph to telecommunications, sharing information has accelerated change and bettered lives. So powerful is access to information that in the hands of the masses it can become the stuff of revolution. It even changes what revolution looks like. Limiting access to information and using propaganda allowed Soviet bloc countries to control their citizens—that is until technology advanced to the point where political barriers could not hold it back. People began to understand their world beyond propaganda and walls came down—figuratively and literally. Access to information changes the world.

That is where we are at today. Around the globe, information is power and access to that information has shifted who has the power. Because of the World Wide Web, the power belongs to the individual. This shift is so profound that the 2006 Time Magazine Person of the Year was—you (Grossman, 2007)! You—the individual connected with the power of many.

It's a story about community and collaboration on a scale never seen before. It's about the cosmic compendium of knowledge Wikipedia and the million-channel people's network YouTube and the online metropolis MySpace. It's about the many wresting power from the few and helping one another for nothing and how that will not only change the world, but also change the way the world changes. (Grossman, 2007, p. 40)

A changing global landscape is being driven by access to unlimited information and the ability for the people to form communities of shared purpose where the cumulative effects of small contributions of many individuals can create a huge collective force. The individual is empowered as never before in world history.

The power of the individual represents the tip of the iceberg of other significant, related shifts. For instance, people are not as aligned to institutions as they were in the past. Today, people have a lot more choices in every aspect of their lives. In previous generations, governments and institutions possessed information that individuals did not, and people found comfort in yielding to the authority of an expert.

Corporations and social institutions that do not respond to the new obligation to release power outward will find themselves rejected in the marketplace and the ballot box. As we move into the 21st century, and technology taps the awesome potential talent of the penumbra of nearly five billion previously disfranchised intelligences on the planet, the Paleolithic concept of single-issue, top-down leadership needs to be redefined. (Burke, 2002, pp. 192–193)

Long gone are the times when patients blindly trusted whatever their doctor told them, or when voters trusted their elected representatives to act altruistically with the people's best interests in mind, or when parents backed what the teacher said instead of defending their child's actions. In each of these examples, access to information was the key component; people trusted those who knew more than they did. The doctor had access to information that the patient did not, the elected officials had information that the average citizen did not, and the teacher had knowledge about teaching and learning that parents did not have.

We are living in a very different age—an age where access to information is in the hands of the individual. Those who have it are empowered to make informed decisions about their lives. Today, many patients will go to the doctor with an idea about what their condition may be. An online search has helped them arrive at an understanding of the possible causes and treatments for their malady.

Open-records laws and the power of the Internet have also empowered citizens. This is a world where the Internet, social networks, blogs, and

YouTube can exert inordinate influence in shaping politics, public opinion, and thinking.

Today, parents of school-age children, as do consumers everywhere, possess a richer sense of their importance than parents of a decade ago. They recognize that whether it be a retail store, bank, hotel, doctor, or school they are being offered a service and their position to that business is important. The consumer is king—and school parents are consumers. The power of the individual is having a profound effect on schools; it drives both the students in them and the parents who send their children there.

Today both students and parents expect, and in fact often require, that the system of education meet their needs. They both have little tolerance for participating in schools that expect them to fit the system. In the past, schools saw students as the ones that needed to adjust to the "way things are done around here." Today, parents show their disapproval of such schools by placing their children in other schools. Students show their disapproval by checking out educationally—just putting in their time. Either way, the individual is exercising control and the educational system loses some of its vitality each time that type of choice is made. This is an age where the power of decisions belongs to the individual, and institutions are expected to adjust to that.

> Today both students and parents expect, and in fact often require, that the system of education meet their needs.

We are living in an age where technology and learning are inseparably linked. Additionally, students today are used to accessing information very differently than the adults in charge of schools. Prensky (2001) refers to the students who are in our schools today as digital *natives*. The teachers and administrators are digital *immigrants*. Technology is integrated into students' being; it is who they are—it is their language. For the rest of us, as immigrants, we are learning a "language" that we were not born with—it is a secondary way of thinking. The Internet, smartphones, text messaging, instant messaging, MP3 players, and digital images are as much a part of these students' lives as the air they breathe. This is how they communicate and stay connected with their networks of friends. This is how they learn. As digital natives, students today are demanding first-hand information about the world. They are getting it through blogs, wikis, searches, twitters, and direct communication with others around the globe. They are using and creating information through a variety of social networking sites and other vehicles such as YouTube. Students want direct contact with the world; they have little tolerance for sitting in a classroom with low levels of technology and having the world filtered and interpreted for them by a digital immigrant that does not understand how they learn.

TAKE A MOMENT

As you consider your district, what policies or practices are in place about students bringing technology into schools to assist learning? Do the policies see students' personal technology as a threat to learning or as an integral part of learning? Do these policies and practices support learning for digital natives?

Accelerating Technological Advancement

Steve Jobs (2006), cofounder of Apple, believes that "innovation distinguishes between a leader and a follower." Innovation in technology is redefining what it means to lead. As has been true throughout history, technology is the catalyst for the global changes we all experience on a daily basis. We know that the devices we use every day seem to morph into something else right before our eyes. Once we figure out a new technology, we wonder how we ever got along without it because it makes our lives easier. Yet the technology that will shape our future will do far more than make our lives easier. The technology on the horizon will change who we are. As profound as that may sound, perhaps more challenging is that the technology to change who we are will be in use before we collectively are able to determine the ethics of its use.

> A tsunami is unnoticeable in the open ocean—a long, low wave whose power becomes clear only when it reaches shore and breaks. Technological revolutions travel with the same stealth. Spotting the wave while it's still crossing the ocean is tricky, which explains why so few of us are aware of the one that's approaching. (Kahn, 2006, p. 100)

The approaching wave that is changing everything is nanotechnology. It will make previous technological advances (even the computer revolution) seem small by comparison. *Nanotechnology is the ability to manipulate matter at the molecular and atomic level.* This ability to engineer molecular systems will affect every aspect of our lives. The first

> The potential of nanotechnology is so massive that it will change much about our world and how we live and learn.

wave of nanotechnology influence is on us now and will grow to be an integral part of our being in the decades ahead. Right now, nanotechnology affects the manufacturing of polymers from computer chips to sunscreens and will soon drive advances in pharmaceuticals, preventive health monitoring, and treatment of diseases.

In the next decade, nanotechnology will involve nanomanufacturing by using nanorobots and nanomachines on the scale of molecules. The result will be a manufacturing revolution.

> Nanotechnology matters because familiar materials begin to develop odd properties when they're nanosize. . . . Not all nanosize materials change properties . . . but the fact that some do is a boon. With them, scientists can engineer a cornucopia of exotic new materials, such as plastic that conducts electricity and coatings that prevent iron from rusting. (Kahn, 2006, p. 100–101)

The downside of nanotechnology is that it is developing far faster than our ability to wrestle with the ethics and implications of its advancing wave. The materials and manufacturing techniques used in nanotechnology are relatively inexpensive. The size of the particles involved means that they can easily pass through skin and tissue. Their toxicity is not known. Overall, there are likely to be environmental, economic, social, and military implications associated with the advancement of nanotechnology (Kahn, 2006). Yet as often happens with accelerated technological advancements, the enormous potential outweighs possible downsides. The potential of nanotechnology is so massive that it will change much about our world and how we live and learn.

The U.S. government understands the importance of getting ahead in nanotechnology. Nearly one and one-half billion dollars was funded for nanotechnology in the 2009 budget (National Nanotechnology Initiative, 2009a) in hopes of positioning businesses and industries to take advantage of a market with exponential possibilities. The scope of nanotechnology's impact is so large that "The worldwide workforce necessary to support the field of nanotechnology is estimated at two million by 2015" (National Nanotechnology Initiative 2009b, ¶ 1).

Driving the development of nanotechnology will be applied mathematics and science. These fields will take on enormous importance in the emerging age of nanotechnology. Additionally, driving the future of this technology will be imagination. The ability to envision what does not yet exist; putting together previously unrelated ideas in new ways will be every bit as important as a strong math and science background. This means that developing students with a strong math and science foundation as well as abilities to think divergently will be very important not only to the individual student but also to the development of a resurgent global economy based in nanotechnology. What are the implications for creating divergent thinkers in a system designed in the Industrial Age when compliance and convergent thinking were valued?

TAKE A MOMENT

Technological advancement means that science, math, and imagination are the keys to the future. Are our students ready for that future? The potential impact of these future trends on our lives will be astounding. Every aspect of our lives will be affected—will your school be affected as well?

The Changing Nature of Work and Global Competition for Jobs

Access to information and accelerating technology has also shaped the work people are doing, how the work gets done, and who is doing the work. Thomas Friedman's (2005) bestseller *The World is Flat* documents the interrelationship of forces that have caused the global economic landscape to increasingly become a more level playing field where shift happens at light speed. Friedman outlines a number of separate events that combine to create a dynamic world environment where linked software, digital advancements, powerful networks, and inexpensive fiber-optic cable make ideas, instead of political power, the global economic dynamo. Friedman's work has brought a new awareness to trends around the globe and their potential to dramatically impact the American way of life.

At the heart of this awareness is how the nature of work is changing. The change in work is an outgrowth of events in the 1990s when favorable legislation and financial boom meant telecommunications companies laid hundreds of thousands of miles of glass cable around the globe. A large global fiber-optic network and the sell-off of telecommunications companies as the financial boom ended meant that digitized data could be sent anywhere around the world at very low costs. Friedman also points out that added to this were advances in the development of workflow software that make it possible for people to communicate with one another using very different software packages. All of this means that work in digital form can be sent anywhere in the world. Advances in technology mean that more work can be digitized now and the competition for who does that work has expanded.

Workers from India, China, and other Asian countries are on the rise, as they are reading your CAT scans, preparing your taxes, and doing investment research for your investment firm. This represents a mere scratching of the surface of the highly skilled work that is done at a lower cost than can be done by American workers. Anything that can be digitized can be sent around the world at very low cost via fiber-optic cable. This means that lots of routine work can be done by highly educated workers in foreign countries.

Accelerating the exodus of American work to workers in other countries is the wage difference between foreign and U.S. workers. For example, "Today, Indian engineers make $7,500 a year against $45,000 for an American engineer with the same qualifications. . . .Why would the world's employers pay us more than they have to pay the Indians to do their work" (National Center on Education and the Economy, 2007, p. xvii)? The impact is that our students are not just competing for jobs with their classmates; they are competing with highly educated people from all over the world. Davis and Stephenson (2006) place this dynamic in perspective:

> The increasing integration of global labor markets, however, is opening up vast new talent sources. The 33 million university-educated young professionals in developing countries is more than double the number in developed ones. For many companies and governments, global labor and talent strategies will become as important as global sourcing and manufacturing strategies. (p. 2)

It is important to point out that the vast numbers of university-educated people educated in the world's two largest education systems, India and China, does not mean that their systems compare to the United States system of education in percentages of university-educated people or in overall quality at the present time. Percentages aside, it is the sheer number of well-educated people and their strong desire for education as a means of creating a better life that should demand our attention.

> The high level of competition for entry into the Indian Institutes of Technology, the Indian Institutes of Management, and other top institutions is enough to spur millions of students to achieve at remarkably high levels, particularly in the areas of science and mathematics. (Cheney, Ruzzi, & Muralidharan, 2005, p. 1)

Imagine the potential shifts caused by 33 million highly motivated university-educated young professionals in countries that have not been a part of the 20th century's global economic and political elite. This is particularly significant when you consider that the standard of living in these countries means that individuals can create a good life working for wages well below those of workers in developed countries. Once one also understands that the work these workers can do is easily digitized and inexpensively sent overseas, then he or she can comprehend the advice that Friedman (2005) passes on to his children, "My parents used to say to me, 'Tom, finish your dinner—people in China and India are starving.' My advice to you is: 'Girls, finish your homework—people in China and India are starving for your jobs'" (p. 237).

TAKE A MOMENT

What do you notice about the changing nature of work around you—in your state? In your community? In your family? How ready are your students to move into a world where the raw material for work is ideas and asking questions that were not asked before?

TWO TRENDS: GETTING BETTER AND BECOMING DIFFERENT

These are only several trends of many. At this point, it is not essential to account for all trends in the external environment. Nor is it important to focus on responses to these trends right now. The important thing is to realize that trends change the context of the work educators do to prepare students for the future. A shifting external environment begs questions such as the following: When we consider what this trend means, is what we are doing now still relevant to preparing students for the future?

Preparing for the future is more challenging than ever before because the world is shifting and evolving new concepts at an incredible speed. Improvement is vitally important, but it alone is not sufficient for helping schools maintain relevance with the external environment.

Not only is it that external trends are changing what our students will need to know, do, and be in the future; what is just as important is how these changes are occurring—and how to keep pace with them. When information is available to everyone and not just an elite aspect of a society or organization, potential energy exists. When the potential energy of information meets imagination, new possibilities arise—often suddenly and unpredictably. This formula is present at a time around the world when more and more people have the ability to focus their time and energy beyond mere day-to-day survival—and when these people can be connected to like-minded others anywhere in the world, a cauldron of infinite possibilities emerges.

What happens is that new ideas create change outside of corporate or institutional channels. In the past, change generated in these channels dominated the world's progress. In these channels, change is planned, strategized, and carefully implemented. It is designed to be incremental and predictable. Although these techniques are still beneficial for managing change, organization leaders must understand that a lot of what is driving societies is change occurring through open access to information fed into self-organized networks that are connected on large scales around the world. These are people-to-people connections unfettered by institutions, governments, or organizations. Change in this realm occurs in adaptive leaps, not incremental steps.

School leaders at all levels are caught in this gap. They are trained to respond to changes through planned strategies and incremental steps. And they are trying to apply these methods in a world driven by networks of people independent of institutions creating potential energy that leads to changes occurring suddenly and unpredictably.

The fundamental premise of this book is that educators face a national, perhaps even global, dilemma. Enormous pressure is placed on educators around the world to improve their systems. The dominant leadership technique is designing incremental improvement—precisely at the time when the world is changing in leaps. This changes the game and challenges schools to become different, not just better. The dilemma is that this type of change requires that leaders understand how to interpret trends and know how to leap—while their systems value incremental improvement. This kind of leadership, the ability to become different, is what we call innovative leadership. It comes from very different thinking than does incremental improvement. It is time that educational leaders looked beyond leading for incremental improvement to creating the conditions for innovative leaps—and that is what this book is committed to help you do.

Redecorating Versus Remodeling

A simple analogy that helps to clarify the difference between improvement and innovation is to think of the difference between redecorating and remodeling. When one redecorates, he or she may change the wall color, put down new carpet, add new furniture, bring in new accessories—but the underlying structure stays the same. When one remodels, things can be very messy for a while because the structure changes before the room can be decorated. The old structure is altered so that something not present before can become part of the home. In redecorating, the elements inside the room structure change; in remodeling, old structures are torn down so that new, better structures can take their place. Improvement is like redecorating; changes are made in the current structure of the system. Innovation is like remodeling; the old structure is altered so that a new one, which better meets the needs of the system, can take its place.

TAKE A MOMENT

What are the curricular and instructional emphases in your schools today? Are they preparing our students for the world they will inherit and need to shape? What, if any, curricular and instructional emphases need to be addressed so our students are capable of leading and prospering?

SUMMARY

Schools have always been future oriented. Their responsibility is to prepare students to lead productive lives through the acquisition of knowledge and by creating the context for how to use that knowledge productively. From the beginning of civilization right up to the present, the well-being of every society depends on the present generation preparing the next generation with the knowledge, skills, attributes, and values necessary to move society forward.

Presently, our global society is one where change is occurring at an ever-accelerating pace. We are faced with the reality that the pace will only be increasing as the future unfolds. The challenge for educators is that these changes are occurring in the environment that is external to schools, yet what happens there affects the relevance of what is taught in schools and how students learn. It is important for educators to look beyond the current capacity of their educational systems and scan the horizon for signs of what the future may bring. Accounting for the challenges of such futures is important new work for school leaders.

In this chapter, we presented several trends that will shape the future of schooling. It was not the intent to create a comprehensive, all-inclusive list for leaders to check off and feel secure that they have the bases covered. The idea is to disturb one's present level of comfort. Our target was to disturb the thought pattern that suggests that the future is an incremental derivative of the past. Many of our current leadership expectations ask leaders to measure present levels of performance and to design interventions to improve performance levels. Our belief is that such methods are good, yet they do not account for the fact that what works today may be irrelevant tomorrow. Being uncomfortable is the beginning of the process that opens individuals and organizations to meaningful change—change that is connected to adapting with the external environment.

Seeing discomfort as an ally is not something leaders have been trained to accept. Most leaders have not been taught how to lead in an environment where uncertainty is a catalyst for building greater organizational capacity. In fact, most have been taught to keep problems to a minimum, avoid confrontation whenever possible, and not air the district's "dirty laundry" for the public to see. Today's world requires leaders to create systems capable of adapting to changes in the external environment. Learning to lead in a dynamic environment has now become a crucial skill for educators. The first step of such leadership relies on opening up to the dynamics of the external environment.

Looking at Your Leadership

In this chapter, we have pointed to trends in the external environment and advocated that for schools to remain vital, their leaders need to create the conditions where their organizations can become different as well as better. To do this will require leaders to rethink some of the practices that form the foundation of their leadership. How ready are you to do so? In this book, our intent is to help you envision new possibilities for leadership so that schools can both get better and become different. On the following page is a quick self-assessment that highlights some of the concepts where shifts in thinking will need to occur. Mark on the line between the concepts where your leadership is now. You may also want to fill in this assessment for how you perceive the leadership of another person you are familiar with, as a means for thinking beyond your own experience to the leadership you observe in your environment. Consider this a snapshot of where you are now. We will revisit this and similar assessments later in the book so that you can watch for shifts in your thinking.

TEAM CONVERSATION STARTERS

Some of you may be reading this book as a team or study group. If so, you may want to create dialogue and discussion around the following questions:

- What sources do we use outside of our own organization to really understand what is driving the economy, politics, and viewpoints of our local community, our state, our nation, and our world? What other sources might we use? If you do not yet look outside your organization to understand these issues, how can you get started?
- What mind-sets, beliefs, needs, and influences are driving the status quo thinking in our organization? Who holds these mind-sets? What would the people in our organization consider innovative? What would really be innovative?
- Who do we need to bring around the table to begin the conversation about what direction our district/school needs to take to bring all of our students to success in the world they will inherit? (Note: It is too early to set up such a meeting now—but it is not too early to envision it.)
- What one question could create divergent thinking at such a meeting?

Self-Assessment

Schools in a Changing World

How do you prefer to create change in your work environment?	Incrementally ♦—♦—♦—♦—♦—♦	In leaps
How do you as a leader react to disturbances to the status quo?	Minimize them ♦—♦—♦—♦—♦—♦	Amplify them
What do you try to provide for your teams as they go about their work?	Structure ♦—♦—♦—♦—♦—♦	Freedom
What kind of instruction do you think will most improve student learning?	Standardized ♦—♦—♦—♦—♦—♦	Customized
What most helps people know what is important in your organization?	Directives ♦—♦—♦—♦—♦—♦	Relationships
How do you prefer information to move through your organization?	Controlled ♦—♦—♦—♦—♦—♦	Free flowing
What type of problem solving do you use when you analyze data?	Convergent ♦—♦—♦—♦—♦—♦	Divergent

Improvement Is Not Enough

2

If you want to be a true professional and continue to grow . . . go to the cutting edge of your competence, which means a temporary loss of security. So whenever you don't quite know what you're doing, know that you are growing.

—Madeline Hunter, American educator

Insanity is doing the same thing over and over again and expecting different results.

—Albert Einstein

IN THIS CHAPTER

In recent years, educators at the local, state, and national levels have focused on improving student achievement—the perennial top priority of public concern. States and school districts have established rigorous academic standards, assessments, and accountability measures—a concerted effort that has involved thousands of educators, employers, and community members nationwide. Schools have responded with strategies to improve teaching and learning. However, a profound gap remains between the knowledge and skills most students learn in school and the knowledge and skills they need in typical 21st century communities and workplaces. (Partnership for 21st Century Skills, 2002, p. 3)

Developing students who will be successful in the world of tomorrow means that it is not enough to improve only the current education system.

We must also realize that new approaches to education are necessary to achieve long-term success. Many of the problems educational leaders face today cannot be solved by doing what we have always done. Knowing when to solve problems from current capacities and knowing when to go into the unknown to seek new capacities is an important new skill required of every leader.

Today's world of rapid change and technological advancement means that, for most organizations, survival requires living on the edge of innovation. Schools are no different. The important challenge facing school leaders, at all levels, is to realize that improving *and* innovating are both necessary and that both need to be a part of their leadership repertoire.

TAKE A MOMENT

What is the goal of education? Of learning? What will students need from schools to ensure students' personal success 10 years in the future? 20 years? Based on your current understanding, what does improvement mean? Based on your current understanding, what does it mean to innovate?

AWAKENING TO THE DIFFERENCE BETWEEN IMPROVEMENT AND INNOVATION

Bob had an experience that dramatically shaped his understanding of improvement and innovation. It took place at the 2005 National Math Symposium. This symposium brought together a group of leading figures in the field of elementary mathematics education. It was held at the Skywalker Ranch, just north of San Francisco. The Skywalker Ranch is nestled in the hills of Nicasio, California. It is the headquarters for Lucasfilms and Skywalker Sound. It is a fabulous 4,000-acre facility that incorporates the home of movie producer George Lucas along with production facilities for his film companies. It also serves as a guest residence for many visitors and is a place where artists and producers come to dialogue about their craft. It is a stunning place to hold a conference, and one feels fortunate, indeed, to participate. The purpose of the symposium was to exchange information, research, and ideas about the subject of teaching and learning math. It was billed as being an event where current research and practice could be featured.

Throughout the day, nationally respected speakers presented research and ideas about improving mathematics instruction for all students. The presentations were thought provoking, and the conversation with other participants was engaging. The unintended interplay of two of the presentations caused a significant disturbance for Bob. This created a reaction that catalyzed the thinking and research we had been doing as a background for this book.

During the day, the focus was on improving mathematics instruction. The theme was in every presentation and on everyone's mind. Although the approaches were different, the one thing everyone agreed on was the need for improvement. One of the speakers was Dr. Joseph Conaty, Director for the Academic Improvement and Teacher Quality Programs Unit, in the U.S. Department of Education's Office of Elementary and Secondary Education. Dr. Conaty spoke about the successes of the No Child Left Behind (NCLB) legislation and the challenges faced by those working to improve the education system. He demonstrated the improvement achieved by NCLB with a graph that showed performance over time. The graph featured lines with an inclined slope to the right. All who could see it recognized this slope as representing steady progress.

At one point, Dr. Conaty displayed a slide that highlighted student performance for various ethnic groups. The data startled Bob. In fact, he was sure the information had set off an alarm throughout the facility. In reality, the alarm was going off inside Bob's head. The seismic disturbance within him knocked his thinking off balance. He longed to stop the presentation and talk about the information on the slide. He refers to this type of learning moment as "knocking the books off the shelf." New information comes in the mind and collides with the present state, upsetting the comfortable patterns of ideas. The ideas no longer fit together the same way, which causes one to look at his or her understanding with a new perspective. Bob welcomes these moments because he notices that these "collisions" and "off the shelf" moments are often the precursor to deep, new insight.

Dr. Conaty's slide showed the performance of eighth-grade students on the National Assessment of Educational Progress (NAEP) mathematics testing. The lines on the graph were sloping nicely to the upper right, indicating that things were improving. Yet Bob was startled by the overall low performance of students across ethnic groups. It was alarming how little the student performance had improved over time. Comparing the present levels of performance to the NCLB targets makes it even more alarming. The data in Figure 2.1, from the National Center for Education Statistic's (2008) Web site, which shows the achievement levels of public school eighth graders, is similar to that presented by Dr. Conaty.

| Figure 2.1 | Mathematics: Percentage of Eighth-Grade Students Proficient or Above by Ethnicity on NAEP Test |

2007	Ethnic Group
41%	**White**
11%	**Black**
15%	**Hispanic**
49%	**Asian/Pacific Islander**

The data displayed in Figure 2.2 from the National Center for Education Statistics (2008) again is comparable to that presented by Dr. Conaty and shows the percentage of eighth graders performing at or above proficiency in mathematics as 15 years of progress compared to where NCLB legislation requires schools to be by 2014.

| Figure 2.2 | Mathematics: Over Time Comparison of Percentage of Eighth-Grade Students at or Above Proficient by Ethnicity on NAEP Test |

1992	2007	2014	Ethnic Group
25%	41%	100%	**White**
2%	11%	100%	**Black**
6%	15%	100%	**Hispanic**
43%	49%	100%	**Asian/Pacific Islander**

The questions were firing rapidly in Bob's mind: "What does it mean to improve the present level of performance?" "What is the target level of improvement in three years? 25%? 60%?" "Why is this data used in a presentation about improvement?" "How can we expect to improve to 100% by 2014?" "Let's not improve it—let's try something different."

Bob is not sure he heard much of what was said by the speakers that followed. He was becoming more and more upset about the continuing presenters' mind-sets of "improvement."

Near the end of the day, a presentation by two Lucasfilms employees created a stark contrast to what the other presenters had been saying. These two men had worked on the movie "Star Wars Episode III: Revenge of the Sith." They spoke to the group about how the movie had been made, and to illustrate their work, they showed scenes from the movie in various stages of production. Their presentation was not really about math, but it was a truly magnificent look at behind the scenes of how the movie was made—and more important, how their organization works. Inspired by George Lucas's directive to the production crew to "put everything, including the kitchen sink, into this one," the two presenters spoke of the way they worked as a team and how ideas turned into new production techniques. It was very clear that the making of each new movie in the Star Wars series meant that all involved stretched to break the mold from previous productions. Each subsequent movie was not just improvement—it was innovation.

New techniques were continuously developed from the belief that the old way wasn't good enough. Everyone involved knew that he or she needed to adopt a new twist to an old adage: *If it's not broken . . . break it.* It was clear that a new production meant that they were going to stretch the realm of possibility so that they would encounter production problems that they could not solve using old methods. It seemed that, when encountered, those moments were welcomed and celebrated. Welcomed because it was a time to break apart the old way and invent a new one. To Bob, this was very different from improvement. This was innovation.

The image that he could not get out of his mind was that at the Skywalker Ranch, a place that exemplified innovation, the best educators could do was to talk about improvement. Somehow, improvement didn't seem to be enough.

IMPROVEMENT IS NOT ENOUGH

It is easy to point out that it is not enough to focus on only improvement. The real issue is how can we create schools that use discomfort and uneasiness to become truly innovative? Intuitively and intellectually, educators, even those who are the most supportive of past methods, know that the students of today already live in a world vastly different from the one where their parents and teachers were raised.

The preceding story illustrates the difficulty educators face every day, as they diligently work to change the outputs of the long-standing system of American education. Educators are working extremely hard to make the current education system better. Yet in many ways, to be responsive to a changing world, there are things that need to be done differently. The difficulty in doing both improvement and innovation stem from the perception of what educational leaders are working on. To many leaders, the work is about improving student performance. Although that is the correct outcome of their efforts, we believe it is the wrong starting point. It is our belief that the work is about facilitating improvement initiatives and leading innovating endeavors that transform the *system* of education, which leads to improved student performance.

Creating the Conditions for Innovation

For many educational leaders, creating the conditions that allow for an innovative public education system seems impossible, so they continue to enforce and reward approaches that succeeded in the past, hoping to prepare the students for their future.

> We need to develop a new language of improvement that is better designed to respond to the problems of the present and lead into the future, rather than one that is designed around the solution of problems belonging to an age gone by. (Clarke, 2000, p. 48)

When we say that improvement is not enough, we have chosen our words carefully. It is important to point out that improvement is an important activity, vital to the health and well-being of every organization. To improve means "to enhance in value or quality: make better." (Merriam-Webster's Online Dictionary, 2009) Isn't this what we are after, to create better quality public schools? Who could argue against that? Improvement is vital, yet it is not enough to focus on *only* improvement.

According to Merriam-Webster's Online Dictionary (2009), to innovate means, "to make changes: do something in a new way." Management guru Peter Drucker defines innovation as "change that creates a new dimension of performance" (Drucker quoted in Hesselbein, Goldsmith, and Somerville, 2002, p. 1). So what we find is that improvement is about getting better; innovation is about *doing things in a new way to achieve results unobtainable by improvement in the current operating paradigm.* Educational leaders must understand that we need both: We need to get better, *and* we need to do things in new ways that change our expectations of what is possible.

To develop a deeper understanding of these leadership concepts, it is important to recognize that there are subtle—yet powerful—differences in what leaders do when they lead for improvement and when they lead for innovation. What one does when he or she is improvement oriented is to strive to get better in the existing standards of practice. Currently, educators seek to improve math scores, for example, by examining data regarding present levels of student performance. Analysis of that data is used to prescribe interventions and set performance goals for the students. There is nothing wrong with that as long as we accept the fact that we are not challenging the boundaries of the currently accepted practices. We are choosing to get better within our current boundaries of practice. We are choosing to improve within the existing paradigm of education.

Looking Beyond Existing Practice

Being innovation oriented means that one is looking for ways to develop new capacities. When an educator is innovation oriented, he or she is open to questioning the validity of the existing paradigm and its effect on enhancing teaching and learning. He or she is also willing to look outside existing practice for those new ways. The working definitions of improvement and innovation are similar to the concepts of single- and double-loop learning introduced by organizational theorists Argyris and Schön (1978), first- and second-order change introduced by Marzano, Waters, and McNulty (2005), and technical problems and adaptive challenges described by Heifetz and Linsky (2002).

Single- and Double-Loop Learning

Single-loop learning involves looking for strategies in the governing variables (Argyris & Schön, 1978). This is the scope used when change is improvement oriented, looking for solutions to current deficiencies within the existing variables. According to Argyris and Schön, double-loop learning involves questioning the validity of the variables before developing strategies of action. This means challenging the underlying assumptions of a situation and understanding the limitations these boundaries place on current actions before developing a solution. In schools, whenever a student is not learning and a teacher challenges the assumption that the *student* needs to be fixed, double-loop learning is possible.

First- and Second-Order Change

Marzano, Waters, and McNulty (2005) introduce the concept of first- and second-order change as two important factors that underlie 21 responsibilities of school leaders. "First-order change is incremental. It can be thought of as the next most obvious step to take in a school or district. Second-order change is anything but incremental" (p. 66). They associate first-order change with single-loop learning and second-order change with double-loop learning and use Argyris and Schön's (1978) concepts to describe the difference between first- and second-order change.

> Single-loop learning occurs when an organization approaches a problem from the perspective of strategies that have succeeded in the past. . . . In a sense, then, single-loop learning teaches us which of our current set of strategies works best in different situations. Double-loop learning occurs when no existing strategy suffices to solve a given problem. In these situations, the problem must be conceptualized differently or new strategies must be conceived. Double-loop learning, then, expands an organization's view of the world while adding new strategies to an organization's repertoire. (Marzano, Waters, & McNulty, 2005, p. 66–67)

Technical Problems and Adaptive Challenges

Heifetz and Linsky (2002) describe the challenges that leaders face as being in two categories: technical problems and adaptive challenges. The distinction between these two is strikingly similar to how Argyris and Schön (1978) define single- and double-loop learning and how Marzano, Waters, and McNulty (2005) define first- and second-order change. Heifetz and Linsky speak of technical problems as problems where people apply current know-how to develop solutions. Adaptive challenges are those where a new way must be learned to solve the problem. They state that adaptive challenges are addressed through new discoveries and new learning and that they require adjustments in attitudes, values, and behaviors before they can be successful (Heifetz & Linsky). They also speak to the importance of leaders understanding the difference between these two and adjusting their approach to fit the type of challenge. They warn that failing to do so causes trouble for leaders and their organizations. "Indeed, the single most common source of leadership failure we've been able to identify—in politics, community life, business, or the non-profit sector—is that people, especially those in positions of authority, treat adaptive challenges like technical problems" (p. 14).

TAKE A MOMENT

What George Lucas posed to his production company were adaptive challenges—and they approached them as such. Are you approaching educating your students for the future as if it is a technical problem or an adaptive challenge?

To Stay Within Existing Practice or to Go Beyond

The concepts of Argyris and Schön (1978), Marzano, Waters, and McNulty (2005), and Heifetz and Linsky (2002) all delineate an important difference between approaching problems from current knowledge and practices and knowing when to move beyond those practices. Many of the problems educational leaders face today cannot be solved by doing what we have always done; they require solutions that bring to life new learning and new practice. The stakes are higher now for our system of education than at any other time.

Knowing when to solve problems from current capacities and knowing when to go into the unknown to seek new capacities is more important than ever for leaders. We think this is the defining difference between leading for improvement and leading for innovation.

An improvement mind-set is useful but not when there is dynamic uncertainty in the organization's external environment. At times of dynamic uncertainty, when the context and relationship to the external environment are shifting, improvement is not enough. At those times, an

organization has the opportunity to challenge some of its existing practices
to create the conditions for the emergence of new ideas. Innovation comes
from very different thinking than does incremental improvement.
Innovation comes from facing
adaptive challenges. It brings *new*
dimensions of performance that cannot be achieved unless there is
some level of dissatisfaction with

> Innovation looks for solutions beyond the
> boundaries of current practice.

the current level of performance. At the fundamental level, leading for innovation starts with dissonance. It requires positioning an organization so that
there is openness to disturbance. Disturbances are necessary to stretch the
capacity of an organization to generate solutions that lie outside the current
capacity. Dissatisfaction and its accompanying dissonance cause old patterns
of thinking to break apart so that new ones can be formed. Improvement
looks for solutions within current practice. Innovation looks for solutions
beyond the boundaries of current practice. Opening that door to innovation
starts by being dissatisfied with the current boundaries.

Does Continuous Improvement Lead to Innovation?

We often hear the question (you may even be thinking it), "Doesn't
continuous improvement lead to innovation?" It is important to understand that improvement is based in an orientation that creates a strong tendency to look for solutions to problems using existing strategies. Searching
for solutions from within the *known* develops a tendency to apply existing
mental models. (We use the terms *mental model* and *paradigm synonymously*
to mean the deep thought patterns present in one's thinking that explain
and define the parameters of a construct.) Staying in an existing mental
model tends to narrow the improvement orientation, creating a barrier
that blocks leaders from tapping into innovation.

When the relationship to the external environment is shifting, an organization has the opportunity to challenge some of its existing practices and mental models to remain relevant. Such disturbances can stretch an organization
to seek solutions that lie outside the current capacity to solve problems. This
causes old patterns of thinking to break apart and old mental models to be
challenged so that new ones can be formed. Being aware of these conditions
as productive opportunities positions the organization to maintain vitality.
This allows leaders and organizations to access both improvement and innovation as mind-sets in helping their organizations adapt and transform.

So the answer to the question about continuous improvement leading to
innovation is *innovation involves moving into disturbances to break apart old ideas*
so new ones can emerge. If your continuous improvement process incorporates
using data to find ways to knock the current system out of equilibrium, and

leaders are encouraged to move *into* disturbances (not away from them) to seek solutions beyond current capacity, then yes, it can lead to innovation. If it does not, then it will not open the door to innovation.

LORIE'S STORY

Innovation starts when old ways of viewing situations are broken apart or lose their influence so that new ways of seeing can emerge. Lorie had an experience that illustrates this. Several years ago, she visited a high school in northern Wisconsin that was in the process of redefining its vocational education mission and purpose. The principal told her that the vocational education staff, as part of a team with students, parents, and local business people, was rethinking what their vocational programs needed to provide to prepare students for the new century. As part of the rethinking process, the team researched what they wanted their students to know and be able to do in the future, where their students were now with their training, and how they had to change to get to their goal of preparing students for the 21st century.

Before they went out and just bought the latest technologies, team members sought to understand changes in their external environment. They visited local and state businesses to see what competencies students needed to be successful with the technologies businesses were using. They researched ways to develop and implement cutting-edge curriculum to further students' knowledge and proficiencies in using state-of-the-art technological equipment and devices. As the research and visits continued and the new curriculum was being developed, they planned how to remodel their classrooms to embrace their new vision. On her visit to the new technology areas, Lorie was struck by the significance of the changes in the old "shop" areas and the work that had been done to prepare the students in the 21st century. Not only did the students, parents, and business people help clean, paint, construct new walls, workstations, shelving, and other essential elements for the new state-of-the-art technologies, but also their ownership and sense of pride in the new mission was enormous.

Through this process, they began to think differently about their purpose. One of the ways that was most visible was in the mat outside the entry to the new *technology* area. It used to be the mat that students cleaned their shoes on before they left the shop area to go into the main hall of the school that read "Please clean your shoes before *leaving* this area." The mat now resides in the main hall, in front of the door to the new technology area with a different message. It now reads, "Please clean your shoes before *entering* this area."

By letting go of their old way of perceiving their purpose, they opened up to the possibility of seeing their challenge as an adaptive one—thus opening up to the possibility of innovation. Had they simply redecorated the shop area, it would have been nice for the students, but their view of learning would not have changed very much. Reperceiving their relationship to the future led

> Please clean your shoes before entering this area.

to seeing things in new ways, which led to the entire remodeling of the area to create and implement a new purpose. In so doing, their view of learning changed significantly, and they were ready to embrace the competencies and proficiencies needed to succeed in the 21st century as adaptive challenges.

What Is Innovative for One May Not Be for Another

As school leaders consider what the disturbances around them mean, they can choose to interpret the meaning within the boundaries of current practice or choose to seek solutions beyond their current practice and mental models. When they open up to possibilities beyond current practice, it can lead to reordering the perception of what is possible and the mental models that create how the school organization operates. This is reordering, moving beyond improvement to the edge of innovation. In the remaining chapters, we will speak in more detail about how this reordering occurs and can be fostered by leaders. As districts find themselves in situations that cause them to look beyond their current know-how, they are opening up to the stages of innovation.

Current practice and existing mental models uniquely affect each district. Therefore, what it takes and what it means to move beyond those barriers is unique to each school and district. As a result, what is innovative to one may not be innovative to another. At this stage, the important point to consider is not what is being produced but that these districts and schools are opening up to the process of reordering.

We think it is important to share stories of this opening up. It is important for two reasons. First, we believe that there are opportunities to open to this process in every school and in every district around the world. We see them around us, and after reading this book, you will see them around you. Rather than look outside to other organizations, we want you to look inward. Overuse of examples of *where it's being done* can lead you to believe that innovation exists somewhere *out there* when, most important, it is right in front of you. Second, nowhere have we found a system that is completely integrating all of what it takes to be innovative—it is too early. These concepts are emerging ones. As times become more challenging, the need to rethink and reinvent becomes more important. So the conditions around schools are just now availing themselves to openness to the concepts of innovation.

Therefore, we want to share with you stories of how districts or schools are beginning to open up to some of these concepts. The most important thing we want our examples to do is to help you answer the following question: How can I develop the conditions in my own system where a culture of innovation can emerge and become the norm along with improvement? Keep in mind that this is not only the work of the leader but also the development of a culture that makes it the work of the whole system.

SCHOOLS WORKING TOWARD INNOVATION

The rest of this book is devoted to creating awareness to the differences between leading for improvement and leading for innovation with the hope of enhancing the capacity of leaders to do both—and more important, to know *how* and *when* to do both. So that your mind can begin to envision what this looks like, the next section presents three vignettes that describe school systems that are opening up to innovate at the same time they are trying to improve.

VIGNETTE 1

MICHELLE'S STORY

Teaching in a big city school, Michelle became frustrated over time at the lack of success students were having and the barriers to her work imposed by command-and-control structures. When she thought of the opportunities she had growing up, something was disturbed inside of her. A dream formed from this creative dissonance. She longed to create a school that had all the "goodies" she had while growing up in suburban schools. Her dream focused on truly meeting the students' academic, social, and emotional needs in a diverse, multicultural learning community. The dissonance between what she was doing and what she wanted to do grew so strong that she acted. Her dream was born when she started her own school. It opened its doors in the fall of 2001 with 23 children in daycare through fifth grade. Today her school is a private school that participates in the city's Parental Choice Program, with more than 700 students in Grades K4–12.

When naysayers tried to dissuade Michelle from starting her school, her passion to make a difference in the lives of children of poverty was amplified. She used that doubt as a motivator. Her vision of what was possible helped her overcome the challenges she faced. Her biggest obstacle was to get students to come to a school that was not yet recognized in the community. Thinking beyond current practice, she recruited students by passing out informational flyers at grocery stores, drug stores, community agencies, festivals, and other places where people gather. Personal contact made Michelle—and what her school stood for—stand out in the community. After a few years, the school created a multimedia campaign on TV, radio, billboards, and on the sides of city buses to promote their school.

In June of 2008, the school celebrated its first high school graduation where Desmond gave a heartfelt speech about his first day at school:

> When I first walked down the halls of the campus as a freshman, I wanted to make an impression on everyone—the teachers, the students, and . . . the ladies! But as I stand before you today, I realize that it is the school that has left an impression on me. I have learned how to be a student, a citizen, and a friend.

Michelle's school built their shared commitment to student success around simple values and then passionately expected everyone involved in the school to live them. The school's passion for caring, respect, and achievement motivated Desmond and his fellow students to succeed. All involved in the school find that being clear about what you, as a "system," stand for and encouraging the freedom to do what is right within those beliefs, allows their school to be valued and respected community-wide. When Michelle reflects on Desmond's words, it gives her the courage and strength to continue her dream to provide excellent education for all students.

Vignette 2

A Midwestern School District

A large school district in the heartland of the United States was undergoing massive change with the closing of schools and the shifting of staff and administrators. With tight budgets and decreasing school enrollment, the district had no other choice. Closing schools and shifting staff is never easy. What is important, however, is that instead of letting this narrow their focus, leadership in this district used it as an opportunity to expand their view. In the midst of all of this professional and personal turmoil, the district recommitted to a focus on quality educational practices. The central office administrators received a state grant and decided to use it to learn more about Assessment *for* Learning and how quality and balanced assessment practices could better prepare their students for the future. The leadership hired an outside consultant to help them in this process.

The first activity was a workshop focused around the vision of quality and balanced assessment and the leadership and teacher competencies that it would take to bring quality and balanced assessment practices into every classroom in the district. Quickly, the central office administrators saw the power of Assessment *for* Learning. They realized that despite what they were dealing with financially they still needed to meet the challenge of preparing their students for future success. They saw Assessment *for* Learning as a leverage point, and they developed a vision of what a quality and balanced assessment system would look like in their district and analyzed what it would take to make the vision a reality. With each step of the process, they would say to one another things such as, "This is huge; it will affect every facet of our organization, yet the potential of what this can do for our students cannot be ignored." "On top of it all, we are in such turmoil right now. We are closing schools, a number of people are losing their current positions, parents are concerned, and students are wondering what building they will be attending next year. Yet the vision of what this could be for our students is compelling." A new vision was just what was needed; the district could begin a new era centered on this new vision.

By the end of the multiday workshop, the central office administrators decided to invite the building leadership to learn more about Assessment *for* Learning. Because it was already May, the building leaders convened with the consultant at the beginning of the following school year.

In the fall, the building leaders and their leadership teams worked with the consultant. Prior to the session, the central office administrators shared their vision and invited the building leadership to learn more and to shape the vision with them. By the end of the workshop, the building leaders and their teams were inspired—thinking beyond their troubling situation to a hopeful future. They were ready to move forward and begin to address what it would take to bring quality and balanced assessment to every classroom for the purpose of increased student motivation and achievement.

This district used disturbances in their situation as an opportunity to bring forth something new—something beyond improvement. Currently, the district and its schools are working on their infrastructure so the system can support people in the pursuit of making the vision of a quality and balanced assessment a reality. The leadership is working hard; all are focused on the vision, and all are addressing what needs to be done, who will be involved, how they will do it, and what resources they need. The administrators and their teams are like an armada of ships moving in the same direction, but each ship has its own dedicated crew and capable captain committed to reaching their destination.

VIGNETTE 3

THE STORY OF SBK HIGH SCHOOL

A large high school located in a suburban area enjoys a reputation for excellence in academics and athletics. It is the pride of the community and recognized in the state for its many achievements. Students perform at a high level on standardized tests, school attendance is high, and school climate is positive.

The high school has worked with its independent kindergarten through Grade 8 feeder schools for the past seven years to ensure a successful transition to the high school in all content areas. As a part of this work, teachers identify what is essential for students to learn, provide evidence of student learning, and share best practices to insure learning.

Recently, the efforts became stuck. Standardized test scores, although high, remain flat. Bringing teachers together, although satisfying, did not lead to significant change in practices to improve student learning. Leaders began to ask the following: What is the

(Continued)

(Continued)

sense of urgency that is driving this work? What changes that are occurring in the learner need to be understood and addressed?

A proposal was made to the eight district administrators to begin a writing initiative with kindergarten through Grade 12 implications. It was at this meeting that the administrators began to question the way things were working and the way learners were being served in the districts.

An outside facilitator was hired to bring together curriculum leaders and superintendents with the intent to examine the current state of interdependence among all of the schools. Statements were drafted that outlined the preferred state and a vision for the future. The Schools for the Future initiative, as it is called, was launched with a vision of the districts collectively adapting to changes in the environment in ways that create relevant, engaging, and self-directed learning opportunities for all students.

One might ask the following questions of a system that was experiencing such success: Why now? What was different? Where was the urgency? SBK High School enjoyed a stable, successful existence focused on excellence for its students. However, disturbances began in little ways that created disequilibrium between and among school leaders. First, 75% of the system's school superintendents were recently hired, and they began to explore the need for new approaches to how they might work together as district leaders. They sought ways they could be more effective in managing district resources. They began to share ways technology could be used to enhance student learning. In these discussions, they also began to share observations about the changing needs of the learner.

It was not until they met with the curriculum leaders and the facilitator that the district administrators made a commitment to move forward to not only improve student learning but also explore what they needed to do in new ways; what they needed to do that was not being done—they needed to innovate. The more the superintendents and curriculum leaders saw change on the horizon and thought about their legacy of excellence, the more they felt compelled to work together to develop new approaches. A deep conviction to provide the best for their students developed, which helped them muster the conviction to act. It took courage to launch the Schools for the Future initiative with the respective school boards and staffs. They knew they needed to help board members and staff understand the urgency facing education in a changing demographic, economic, global, and technological world. It took courage to admit to themselves that they did not yet understand the changing needs of the learner. As leaders who others expected to have answers, it took courage to acknowledge publicly that they did not have the answers—yet. They wanted everyone to understand that as part of the process all would need to learn new ways of thinking. Most important, all needed to trust that what evolved would be meaningful—that just continuing to get better at what they were already doing would not be enough.

The story of SBK High School will be revisited in more detail throughout the book as an illustration of one district's effort to both improve and innovate.

SUMMARY

Improvement is about getting better; innovation is about doing things in a new way to achieve results unobtainable by improvement in the current operating paradigm. Both are important for school organizations. It is necessary to improve and get the most out of current practices. It is just as important to question current practice in light of a changing external environment and, when necessary, shift it to maintain relevance with that environment. This is moving beyond improvement to innovate so that a *new dimension of performance* can be defined.

It is by being unsettled and open to the dissonance between current practice and its relevance that educators open up to moving beyond improvement to the possibility of innovation and enhanced capacity. It is at those times that their organization has the opportunity to challenge some of its existing practices to create the conditions for the emergence of new ideas. What it takes to open up to reordering existing practice is unique to each situation. The important thing is for leaders to help their school organizations take that journey and uncover the unique potential it affords.

To encourage that journey, it is important for leaders to appreciate the difference in the degree of change called for (i.e., the difference between technical problems and adaptive challenges). When that is understood, then there is a better awareness of when to seek solutions from current know-how and when a new way must be learned to solve the problem. This allows leaders and organizations to access both improvement and innovation as mind-sets in helping their organizations adapt and transform.

Perhaps by now, you are questioning whether it is possible to go from 11% proficiency on math scores to 100% proficiency through improvement initiatives alone. You may be wondering how to create the dissonance necessary so that your school staff can begin to look beyond current practices for dynamic solutions to student learning problems. If so, congratulations, you have begun the journey to innovative leadership.

TEAM CONVERSATION STARTERS

If you are reading this book with a team or study group, you may want to explore the following questions together:

- Have our recent efforts to elevate student learning been confined to the improvement side of things or have we pushed through to the innovative side? What has kept us on the improvement side? Or what has pushed us through to the innovative side? If we have not pushed through, what would it take to do so?
- What would be good to do in our classrooms or school to improve student learning but we have not tried because we perceive that it will really rock the boat?
- What are the barriers and opportunities to make it happen?
- What one mental model about teaching and learning is most influential in our improvement efforts? Would that have to change for us to be innovative? If so, how might we start to do that?

Self-Assessment

Improvement Is Not Enough

Through the remainder of the book, we will be helping you develop the capacity to lead for innovation—as well as improvement. To get you started, let's find out where you are now. Below is a self-assessment that can provide a baseline from which to assess your growth. Think back to your leadership behavior and activity over the past few months. How often have these been based in the following mind-sets?

A desire to make things better	Never ♦——♦——♦——♦	Always
A desire to find undiscovered ways	Never ♦——♦——♦——♦	Always
Staying within the current boundaries	Never ♦——♦——♦——♦	Always
Challenging the boundaries	Never ♦——♦——♦——♦	Always
Seeing challenges as technical	Never ♦——♦——♦——♦	Always
Seeing challenges as adaptive	Never ♦——♦——♦——♦	Always
Striving to keep things stable	Never ♦——♦——♦——♦	Always
Moving into instability	Never ♦——♦——♦——♦	Always
Responding to problems through fixes	Never ♦——♦——♦——♦	Always
Working to develop root-cause solutions	Never ♦——♦——♦——♦	Always
Breaking down problems into parts	Never ♦——♦——♦——♦	Always
Seeing interconnected patterns to problems	Never ♦——♦——♦——♦	Always

Attributes of Innovation   **3**

There is no future in vanilla. . . . (The) future belongs to those who know how to make the richest chocolate sauce, the sweetest, lightest whipped cream, and the juiciest cherries to sit on top, or how to put them all together into a sundae.

—Thomas Friedman, Pulitzer prize-winning author

It is . . . easier for leaders to praise innovation in theory than to support it in practice.

—Rosabeth Moss Kanter, author and professor

IN THIS CHAPTER

Improvement has been at the forefront of the educational agenda for some time now. There currently exists a broad base of ideas and practical approaches for how to go about improving student learning. In contrast, there is very little available for leaders to draw from when it comes to seeking knowledge about how to innovate. To begin to develop that understanding, this chapter will present four key attributes that school leaders should keep in mind as the foundation for creating an innovative school culture. A dilemma will be uncovered in that the key attributes needed for innovative school cultures are not strengths fostered by the traditional organizational structure.

The theories developed in science shape our personal views of how the world works and, from that, how we go about creating order in the pieces of our worlds that we manage. As a result, scientific theory underlies how we organize our workplaces. In this chapter, we will briefly discuss the science that forms the basis of two organizational mental models that are presented. Once the thinking behind the mental models is revealed, attention is turned to how to use this understanding to lead schools into the future.

STARTING THE JOURNEY TO IMPROVEMENT AND INNOVATION

In Chapter 1, we asked, what would it look like if the national agenda for schools could be aimed toward seeing them as living systems, with the challenge to help them advance in response to a changing world as opposed to fixing them to make them better? We ask this because seeing educational systems through mechanistic paradigms puts forward a mind-set of fixing. A fixing mind-set has limitations.

Think of it this way. If we owned a vintage automobile, we would want to keep it running in top shape—that would mean that there are times that it may need to be repaired and fixed to improve it. But if we want the latest innovative advancements that the auto industry has to offer, better gas mileage, advanced safety features, long-term body integrity, greater reliability, heated seats, symphonic sound, and much more, we would not try to add these on to our vintage auto. It would not work because the original electrical and mechanical systems were designed for a completely different purpose.

To be able to meet changing customer demands and advancing technology, the auto industry must continually push beyond improvement to innovation. Today, this is more real for the industry than ever before. Automakers are facing huge challenges of relevancy, and their survival hangs in the balance. Improving the gasoline-powered engine can only go so far, but it will not be the answer when the paradigm changes based on demands for cars that run on alternative fuels.

Whether realized, schools are in the same position. Schools provide a service—preparing students for the future. For that service to be relevant, improvement is not enough. At some point, leaders need to look beyond adding the *latest movement* on top of education's vintage system. There is a point when redesign is necessary—and that time is now. Redesign will not succeed through mandates. It will succeed only when leaders roll up their sleeves and move into the challenging work of making their system of education something different than it is now—without abandoning the essence of the system in place. We call this work leading for improvement *and* innovation. It involves knowing when to do which—when to seek solutions within existing practice and when to seek solutions beyond what is currently possible, such as the school Michelle created for multicultural learners in the central city (see Chapter 2).

It involves creating a culture open to innovation—one like the culture at Lucasflims where the challenge is to find ways to bring to screen what has not been possible in the past. In schools, this equates to creating a culture where people see their work as bringing to reality what has not been possible for students in the past.

RANDY'S STORY
LOOKING BEYOND CURRENT PRACTICE

Bringing to reality what has not been possible in the past is a process that involves recognizing something discordant as an opportunity for *double-loop learning, second-order change,* or an *adaptive challenge.* Once recognized, it then involves looking for solutions beyond current capacities and know-how. A student named Randy helped a principal and his staff understand the power of looking beyond what is presently possible.

In his first years as a principal, Rick worked in a small elementary school composed of veteran teachers. The staff was happy and comfortable with whom they were. They were a fun-loving group that enjoyed socializing together, yet they managed to avoid discussions on professional practice. When something occurred that did not square with their operating beliefs, there was no place to discuss the dissonance to use it as an impetus for improving instruction. That meant that, most of the time, such disturbances were subconsciously referenced against a teacher's existing mental model. If it didn't fit in that model, something was wrong in the external environment. For instance, if a child was not as motivated as other students, there must be something wrong with the child. After all, the teacher would surmise, my techniques motivated other students; therefore, my practice works to motivate students. If this child is not motivated, it can't be because of me.

This changed subtly, yet powerfully, one day. A first-grade teacher came to Rick concerned about one of her students. Randy was beginning to shut down; she could see it in his eyes. It was only October, and she could see that Randy was very frustrated. His reading skills were far behind those of the other students—and he knew it. The interventions in the teacher's repertoire were not working, yet she couldn't just dismiss it as something wrong with Randy's life. She couldn't shake those eyes, and the look that she had seen there. She sought out Rick to help her make sense of the dissonance she felt. She needed some new ideas.

(Continued)

(Continued)

Rick and the teacher decided the first step would be to ask Randy's mother to come in for a conference. This was a big step because Randy's mom gave the impression of being one who is difficult to deal with. At the conference, the news of Randy's progress was shared. His mother became teary, saying, "I knew I should have retained him in kindergarten." There it was right there, the easy out. Mom was saying it was her fault.

Empathy drove Rick's response to Randy's mother. Her words had touched him and caused him to say something that surprised him. He said, "We're not saying he can't learn. We are just saying that we haven't found the way to teach him so that he can learn—but we will." After the conference ended, Rick vividly recalls walking down the hallway feeling stunned. His head was spinning, "What did I just say? What have I promised? Why did I say that? I have no idea what to do next?"

That statement led to in-depth conversations with the teacher. It opened both of them to moving beyond their comfort zones. It led to seeking ideas from others, it led to trial and error, it led to deep inquiry, it led to self-doubt and exhilaration, and . . . it led to innovation.

After several weeks of dialogue and discussion, an intervention was designed for Randy. The eventual success of that model led to a reading intervention program at the school, which, within a year, led to the program being in all seven of the district's elementary schools—which eventually impacted the way reading was taught for all primary students. A transformation that would not have been possible if the teacher had not felt a need to have her ideas collide with other ideas so that her dissonance could be resolved. No one intended to change instruction for all students, but the ideas that collided in Rick's office that morning kept colliding and amplifying until the meaning resonated on a much larger scale. Eventually, district leaders could not ignore the meaning that was created. Randy is considered a hero by the first-grade teacher and Rick. They know that he taught them much about what it means to be a professional.

KEY ATTRIBUTES FOR INNOVATION

In the preceding story, Rick and the teacher realized that the solutions for helping Randy were beyond their current know-how. They let their dissonance with Randy's situation take them on a journey that brought to life something not possible previously—and the whole system benefited. Their story illustrates four key attributes necessary for an innovative school organization: (1) disturbance, (2) self-referencing, (3) amplification, and (4) engagement.

- Disturbance is something that perturbs, to any degree, the current state of thinking or being.
- Self-referencing is the process of interpreting the meaning of new information by examining it against existing constructs such as a vision; mission; or set of beliefs, policies, or principles.
- Amplification is the process where an idea gains strength and grows into something whose meaning cannot be ignored.
- Engagement happens when a new idea emerges and competes with existing ideas for a place in current practice.

Disturbance

In writing about the processes living systems use to reorder, Margaret Wheatley (1999a) states, "What is important is that a member of the system chooses to be disturbed. 'Chooses' is the important word here because the freedom to be disturbed belongs to the individual" (p. 3). We like the term *chooses*, and we have seen that the potential for innovation begins when someone *chooses* to be disturbed.

Choosing to be disturbed is the first attribute of innovation. It can take many forms ranging from the look in a student's eyes, to the completion of a research study, to exposure to new ideas in a book, to the innocent comments of a kindergartener. The point is that some thought, action, comment, or anything really catches the attention of individuals or groups and causes them to pause and reflect about what is and what might be. In the preceding story, Randy's teacher chose to be disturbed by what she saw in his eyes. She felt she needed to do more, to take another course of action, rather than accept Randy's difficulties as being part of who he was. She would not accept status quo for Randy.

Choosing to be disturbed is, in our definition, choosing to open up to an experience that perturbs the status quo. In his benchmark book *The Fifth Discipline*, Peter Senge (1990) illustrates the concept of dialogue through a discussion of how physicists interact with one another. The point being that these individuals were confident in their beliefs, yet at the same time, they were willing to let their beliefs be disturbed by other ideas to continuously test their relevance. We have this ideal in mind when we say *choosing to be disturbed*. This disturbance is not a shattering of old ideas, rather a means of nudging our accepted ideas to make one aware of their relationship to other ideas. In essence, this process asks the question, does this belief I hold still have its same meaning in light of this new idea? This process of opening one's understandings to the challenge of new ideas leads to strengthening or rethinking accepted understandings.

Self-Referencing

The second attribute is referencing this reflection against a vision, mission, set of beliefs, or principles: "If we stand for ____, then why do we do ___?" or "___ is a key principle here. Could we get better at that, if we did ___?" or "I'm not willing to accept this as the only alternative." This concept we term self-referencing. How does this new information square against our vision, beliefs, or principles? The question needing to be answered at this point is why am I noticing this information? Ultimately, one wonders if this information can lead, in some way, to something new or better emerging. If it creates a nudge in that direction, then the disturbance creates the potential to activate a motivating sense of purpose. In the preceding story, this stage was activated through Rick's comment to Randy's mother. The school had a stated belief that "all children can learn." The words of the mother caused Rick to reference Randy's situation against that belief. In doing so, the belief statement moved from *words on the wall* to an active reference point. It became a container for discussion and action, not just a statement.

> If it can create enough meaning to cause questioning of existing practice, then the door opens to innovation.

When new information disturbs the status quo, we have three choices: (1) dismiss the information, (2) make the information fit our current constructs, or (3) make our constructs fit the new information. The first two options process the information from the perspective of our unique identity seeking to answer the question, how does this new information relate to me? The third option moves one away from the perspective of unique individual to a more connected self—one that is part of something larger, in this case, an organization with a mission and a profession with a moral purpose. The question being answered here is how does my identity relate to this information? When we ask, why am I noticing this information? it can help us see ourselves in relationship to the information rather than trying to interpret the information to our personal interests. This is why the last of these options is the one that opens us up to innovation, and thus, we choose to let the information disturb us.

The two attributes, disturbance and self-referencing, are not sufficient to create innovation alone. Every reader is able to cite examples where important, significant ideas with great potential to improve learning shined brightly and faded quickly, without leaving a lasting impact. This was because the meaning of the idea's importance did not unseat accepted practice throughout the system. In such cases, the importance of the idea needs to resonate on a systemic level so that it can challenge existing ideas. If it can create enough meaning to cause questioning of existing practice, then the door opens to innovation. The third attribute, therefore, is an amplification of the new idea's meaning on broadening levels. In the preceding story, the teacher and Rick engaged each other in discussions about possible actions to help Randy. They also expanded their circle and engaged others outside of the organization until their ideas grew into a course of action.

TAKE A MOMENT

What ideas have you had that you thought would be good for your classroom or your school and when you tried them they worked quite well? Did you take those ideas to a broader arena such as to your colleagues, the whole school, or the whole district? Why or why not?

Amplification

Amplification is the process by which an idea gains strength. To get to innovation, an idea needs to grow. Such ideas start out as a spark in the mind of an individual or small group. Think back to the seed ideas that sparked Michelle's school, the districts in the vignettes in Chapter 2, and Randy's story. From these early sparks, ideas have to be brought out into the light for others to see. Ideas need to be discussed with others and tested against current practice and current reality. The point of this collision of ideas is to create the circumstances where the new idea knocks one's thinking off balance. To bring it back in balance, one has to examine the old idea for a moment. In this moment, the door is opened to questioning the underlying mental model at the root of the idea.

To survive, an innovative idea must have staying power. It may not win people over right away, but does it stay in their minds and cause them to keep thinking about it? If it keeps nudging their thinking, then people keep coming back to it. Its meaning will change as others interact with the idea—and that is the point. The discussions, interactions, and reflections of everyone create a shared meaning of the idea. If the idea creates enough of a buzz in the networks of the organization, then it is ready for the next phase of innovation. If not, then it fades into the scrapheap of organizational ideas.

TAKE A MOMENT

What in your organization is creating a buzz? What is causing interactions, discussions, and maybe a rippling disturbance among various members of your organization? Why?

Engagement

Engagement is the fourth attribute of an innovative organization. As the importance of an idea grows, its meaning is amplified throughout the system. At this point, the door to innovation is open, but the new idea must engage with existing practice and the mental models individuals possess, which keep existing practice in place. In the preceding story, the engagement stage occurred after new techniques were tried with Randy and results were seen. These results were shared with others around the school district. Skeptics challenged the results, but over time, the district could not ignore what had been accomplished with Randy. The new practice engaged people's mental model about what could be done when teaching reading to remedial readers. Action on a systemic level was at hand.

New ideas need to challenge and compete against existing ideas and either win out over them or fade away. This may sound a lot like survival of the fittest . . . because it is. New ideas need to collide with existing ideas; they need to engage our minds and our hearts. Their meaning needs to change and strengthen through this process until they are so significant that they cannot be ignored. If they cannot survive this process, then they do not deserve to become part of accepted practice. If they can, then innovation is at hand.

> New ideas need to collide with existing ideas; they need to engage our minds and our hearts.

"Few people have had as profound an impact on the theory and practice of social and organizational psychology as Kurt Lewin" (Schein, 2007, ¶ 1) Lewin developed a theory of change processes in human systems that is simple yet profound. His change model identifies three stages: (1) unfreezing, (2) change, and (3) refreezing (Schein, 1999). The essence of this model is that for significant change to occur, the first step is unlearning, the breakdown of meaning or relevancy. That is followed by a change and then the solidification of the new learning. In schools, this means we can impose a new teaching method or instructional resource on teachers, but it will not produce change unless leaders create the opportunities for teachers to let go of, or disconfirm, their current practice. If the current practice is not "unfrozen," then the new practice cannot take root.

Lewin's three stages of change represent the essence of the fourth stage of innovation: engagement. For an idea to create innovation, it must eventually engage the mental model people hold on a systemic level. It must be the catalyst for unfreezing their mental model so that a new one can be formed. If this does not occur, innovation will not happen. This is why so many good ideas—ideas that hold great potential—do not survive to impact student learning. It is not about whether they are better than what is currently being done. Quite simply, they did not unfreeze the mental model underlying the existing practice to begin the process of change.

TAKE A MOMENT

Regarding teaching, learning, or assessing, what, if any, practice underwent unfreezing in your school or district so that a new mental model could be formed and innovation could take place? What caused that to occur? What old mental model would you like to see go through the process of unfreezing? Why? How?

UNWELCOME IN COMMAND AND CONTROL

Disturbances, self-referencing, amplifying, engaging, challenging existing practice, and unfreezing—these attributes may be making you a little uneasy. You may be thinking, "I want to open my organization up to innovation, but those concepts make me uncomfortable. They seem so messy. Isn't there a more controlled way to go about innovation?" If you are thinking along these lines, then this is the perfect time to examine why these ideas make you uncomfortable. These concepts run counter to deeply held theories of how order is formed and how organizations adapt those theories into operating mental models that create the practices used every day to lead and manage people.

One startling conclusion we have reached is that the four attributes of an innovative organization are not welcome in the traditional command-and-control organizational model that serves as the basis for most organizations and almost every school district in our country. Most educators are working in organizations rooted in the desirability of stability and control. Therefore, attributes such as disturbance are seen as something to be diminished, not amplified. Self-referencing creates vulnerability in the command-and-control mind-set and is viewed as unnecessary. After all, policy is the referencing required in the command-and-control organization, not self-referencing. Engagement of ideas can be seen as a loss of efficiency in command and control: The essence of this model is compliance, not engaging for deeper meaning. If new strategies are necessary, they are developed at the top of the organization where the view of the big picture resides.

The obvious question becomes, how do leaders develop the attributes of innovation in organizations that may not welcome them? The answer is found in a journey that starts with examining the underlying paradigm of leadership and checking that paradigm against what systems need today. It involves shifting the vision of leadership to principles more in line with the way people are connecting and working together today. It is a journey where leaders look inward to examine their practice against the needs of an evolving world. And it involves connecting to support one another in the process of leaving one paradigm for another. It is a journey that requires patience and celebration as new capacities develop. To reorder leadership so that systems of education can become innovative as well as improvement oriented is a long, arduous road. It is, however, a road that must be traveled. It is a journey that begins with a first step. That first step is to be open to understanding what underlies the practice of leadership and what works to foster innovation.

> Helping their systems adapt to remain vital is a much more potent image for the work facing educators than is an image of fixing.

TAKE A MOMENT

In your leadership, do you welcome the four attributes of an innovative organization: (1) disturbance, (2) self-referencing, (3) amplification, and (4) engagement? What in your current behavior as a leader indicates that this is so?

ENVISIONING LEADING ADAPTIVE SYSTEMS

A key to starting the journey lies in the Senge, Cambron-McCabe, Lucas, Smith, Dutton, and Kleiner (2000) quote in Chapter 1 about schools. It is the view that schools are not broken but, instead, under stress and need to evolve. This conjures up images of schools functioning as living systems do, as they change and adapt to remain in sync with their surroundings. Helping their systems adapt to remain vital is a much more potent image for the work facing educators than is an image of fixing.

A journey begins with a vision. The vision of leadership that starts this journey is leading a system in a manner that stimulates its adaptation—adjusting to changes in the environment while remaining vital and relevant.

It is not possible to journey toward this vision through a mechanistic mind-set. The metaphors that form that mind-set originate in the scientific worldview of Newton—which drove science for three centuries. This view saw the world as working like a great mechanical clock. It also placed humans in the position of sole interceder; systems wind down unless we are there to reverse that—to wind them up, keep them from decay, and fix them.

Scientific understanding has begun to see the world in new ways. Fortunately for us, there are metaphors in new science that can illuminate the work of leaders trying to help their systems adapt. These metaphors come from developing understanding of how natural systems change and evolve. The place to begin our journey is where the paradigm underlying traditional leadership and the one underlying leadership for adaptation both originate—that place is science.

This book is not about science, and we do not want to over burden the reader or muddy the waters with a lot of scientific theory. Yet it cannot be ignored that science is at the root of our beliefs about how the world works. So to start with, let's take a brief look at how science now sees the way systems adapt to their surroundings.

It's Not Just About Stability Anymore

Without going into a lot of scientific theory, the important thing for leaders to keep in mind is that the science of the Newtonian era emphasized concepts such as determinism, linearity, stability, predictability, and reductionism. These concepts have also become important precepts of classically defined leadership. One of the attractions of the Newtonian paradigm is that it allows us to believe that we have control. It causes us to think we can influence weather and control disease—that we can measure and engineer better student performance, and then all will be well. It also leads us to place an inordinate premium on stability, keeping things from becoming too unbalanced. Stability is often valued to the point where leaders are rewarded for their ability to not let little ripples develop into big waves that rock the boat.

However, over the last half century, through studies in quantum physics, evolutionary biology, and fields such as chaos theory and complex adaptive systems, scientific focus has shifted to the importance of disorder, instability, disequilibrium, and nonlinearity. New science findings point out that living systems maintain an adaptive, competitive edge and coexist with their surrounding systems, by using various states of order.

Stuart Kauffman (1995) has written extensively about these topics and points out that "on many fronts, life evolves toward a regime that is poised between order and chaos" (p. 26).

Contrary to Newtonian theory, scientists now find that for systems to be healthy, "a living system must be able to strike an internal compromise between malleability and stability. To survive in a variable environment, it must be stable, to be sure, but not so stable that it remains forever static" (Kauffman, 1995, p. 73). That some level of instability is an important element of maintaining healthy living systems is a profound shift in thinking from classic science. Remember that the old science view used classic mechanics and a metaphor of a clock to explain the universe. In this view, the world was winding down, and humans were here to stabilize that. New science reveals that the world is not winding down but that natural systems reorder by using instability in a state combining malleability and stability.

It is here that natural systems open to possible adaptation. Classic science defines relationships linearly: where cause and effect are direct and proportional. In the state between order and chaos, a nonlinear relationship is created where it is possible for small fluctuations to trigger evolutionary change. Systems in this state are open to the environment and are filled with small fluctuations, most of which have no effect. At times, however, certain small fluctuations are amplified and grow in importance. Dr. Ilya Prigogine, who received the Nobel Prize in Chemistry in 1977 for his work in the area of thermodynamics, referred to this process as perturbation (Wikipedia, 2008). As the perturbation grows, its meaning may be passed through the networks—continuing its amplification. As energy increases, the system becomes agitated and feedback intensifies. This intensity may become more chaotic, moving the system farther from a state of equilibrium. It is then that the system reaches a defining moment, what Prigogine called a bifurcation point. This occurs when the system, in its present structure, cannot deal with the meaning of the agitation, so either it reorganizes to a higher level of complexity or it disintegrates (Prigogine & Stengers, 1984).

This is a profoundly important shift in thinking that potentially changes the paradigm of leadership. Traditional leaders often view part of their role to be to diminish or quickly dissipate disturbances or disruptions to their systems to keep things on an even keel or calm the waters. This new view says that to be healthy and adaptive there needs to be levels of disruption and disturbance that keep a system off balance—that keep it from becoming too stable. This means that leaders need to rock the boat a bit and disturb the waters.

The true significance of Prigogine's (Prigogine & Stengers, 1984) work is the awareness it creates to healthy systems existing on the edge between order and disorder. Systems avail themselves to getting a jump-start on change by having a strong identity yet being open to new information. "All life lives off-balance in a world open to change. And all life is self-organizing" (Wheatley, 1999b, p. 89).

The state between order and chaos is important for leaders to understand—it is where reordering occurs in living systems and innovation occurs in organizations. But what does organization look like in this state? Central to a system reorganizing in this state is the concept of self-organization.

SELF-ORGANIZING SYSTEMS

In the state between order and chaos, systems are not losing order, but rather they are in the process of reordering through self-organization. "Self-organization is a process of attraction and repulsion in which the internal organization of a system, normally an open system, increases in complexity without being guided or managed by an outside source" (Wikipedia, 2009, ¶ 1).

Systems from biological to organizational are made up of networks of relationships formed around a shared intent or purpose. It is a relationship built on the principle that there is mutual benefit to being connected (i.e., cells in an organism, plants and animals in an ecosystem, students and staff in a school). Earlier, we spoke of these types of systems thriving in a paradoxical state between stability and instability. The paradoxes do not end there. Within the system are individual entities that also exist in a paradoxical relationship. Each entity is an autonomous individual making unique choices and movements and possessing a unique history. At the same time, it is a part of something larger. Each entity has a relationship to the other entities, influencing each other, sharing common constraints, resources, and well-being. The special aspect of this paradoxical relationship is that these entities join together in ways that afford characteristics and advantages that do not belong to any of them (i.e., differentiation), and the whole shapes what is possible for any of the individual entities (i.e., how it thrives). In nature, these networks are molecules that form cells and cells that form organisms and organisms that form ecosystems.

This paradoxical relationship of unique entity connected to a larger whole in a way that benefits both the individual and the whole is a metaphor that excites us as authors. This surely describes what we want for our organizations and is more hopeful and potent than thinking of the people in our schools as cogs in a machine. Figure 3.1 represents this relationship of a self-organizing system.

Figure 3.1   Relationships in a Self-Organizing System

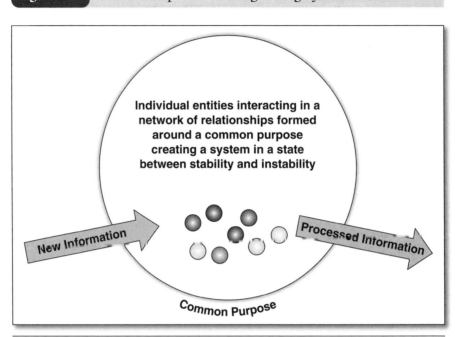

Whether biological or organizational, new information and ideas continuously enter the network and interact with the individual entities, represented by the shaded dots in Figure 3.1. Most of the time, this information passes through the network with little or no attention. Occasionally, a piece of new information catches the attention of one or more of the entities by *disturbing* the status quo. In our bodies, such a disturbance triggers antibodies in response to bacteria. In organizations, it means someone notices something in reference to the vision, mission, or beliefs. When this occurs, the paradoxical relationship of *unique* yet *part of* comes into play. The individual entity not only processes the information based on its unique identity but also it creates meaning and determines the importance of that information by referencing it against the common bond that holds the network together. In essence, the entity is responding to two aspects: (1) What does this new information mean to me? And (2) what does it mean to the system as a whole? This is represented in Figure 3.2.

If the meaning of the new information disturbs the status quo, then it disturbs some aspect of the individual or the individual's relationship to the whole. To make sense of it, the entity must circulate the information through the network and trigger feedback. The meaning of that information changes as it is interpreted by the other individual entities of the network. This dynamic is represented in Figure 3.3.

Figure 3.2 Entity Is Disturbed and Seeks Meaning

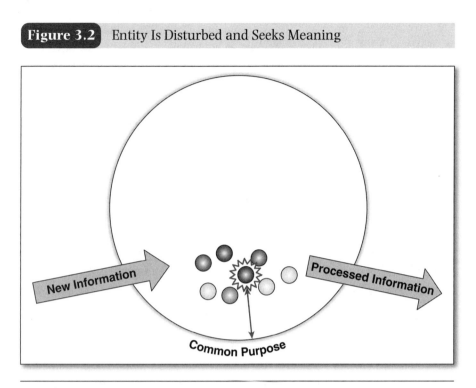

Figure 3.3 Information Circulates Through the Network

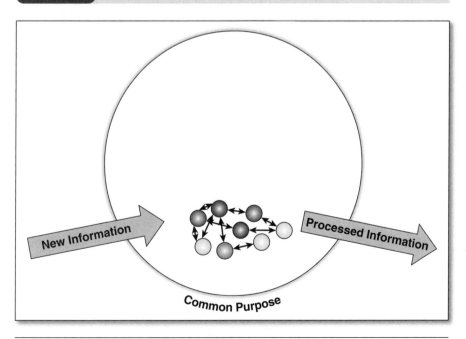

Through this process, the information either grows in importance or diminishes. If the generated collective meaning is important enough, it will cause a reaction—the system must respond. If the system cannot respond in its present structure, then the entities must reorder. This reordering augments the mutuality of the individual entities—the common purpose is enhanced. In this way, the system adjusts and adapts to its environment. The culmination of this self-organizing is represented in Figure 3.4.

We introduce you to the idea of self-organization because the principles are well suited to the four attributes of innovation. Together they offer hopeful, new metaphors for leadership intent on helping schools become adaptive. In self-organizing systems, adaptation and evolution take place because of a strong identity and entities being open to disturbances. In this state, there is an opportunity for small influences to have a large impact. The system is already dynamic and referencing so that there is a context for nonlinear dynamics where small inputs can potentially produce profound changes. In organizations, as we found out in Rick's school, this is a state where innovation can occur—where disturbances are potential energy that are referenced against a clear purpose, where ideas collide with other ideas and are amplified or diminished, and if

Figure 3.4   The System Adapts Through Self-Organization

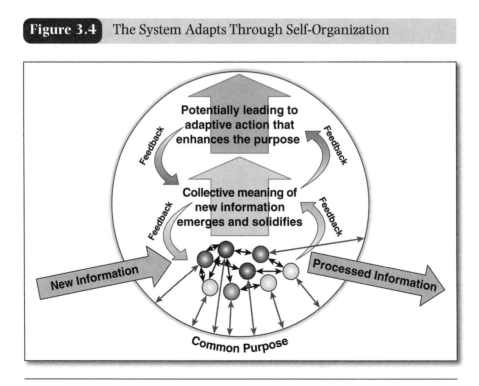

amplified, challenge the status quo—to either replace the current state or not. This is an atmosphere where systems of education can become more relevant and adaptive.

> ## TAKE A MOMENT
>
> In your own words, describe the connection between the old and new science and how these concepts relate to improvement and innovation. Reflect on the extent to which you believe leaders in your organization embrace the new science.

STARTING THE JOURNEY

Self-organization is a form of organization that is demonstrating remarkable effectiveness and efficiency in many sectors across the globe. It is affecting your life, and you may not even realize it. Self-organizing networks explain why individuals, service organizations, or church groups often respond to crises such as September 11th or Hurricane Katrina in a more effective and timely manner than do bureaucracy-laden governments. Such networks of organization are also the catalyst for the wide array of online communities and social networks accessed by millions through the World Wide Web.

The journey to innovative leadership begins by recognizing the limitations of the traditional organization when it comes to innovation and then moving toward a vision of leadership more conducive to innovation. The principles of self-organization hold great potential for creating an organizational environment conducive to innovation—yet the reality is that our organizations are built on the foundation of old science. This would surely seem to create an impossible situation—how do we grow adaptive systems in organizations designed to be stable? The good news is that our thoughts and expectations in schools are already evolving in that direction.

These types of self-organizing networks are evident in schools when the derived meaning of a memo or a rumor moves through the school at the pace of a wildfire. They are also evident as networks of teachers initiate learning teams to collaborate and enhance their practice, without a directive to do so. We also believe that self-organization is a useful model for visualizing the type of learning environment that educators are asked to create today. Today's schools are standards driven. In this environment, teachers are expected to constantly monitor learning data. From that learner feedback, they are expected to tailor unique, individualized strategies to get all students to the same learning outcomes.

Today, we expect teachers to make decisions about the next thing they will teach based on interpreting a continuous flow of information that, at the same time, should be interpreted about each student and the performance of the class as a whole. This shift in expectations is closely aligned to the characteristics of nonlinear, self-organizing definition of learning.

You find such characteristics as nonlinear and self-organizing in the work of those systems implementing Assessment *for* Learning. One of the most compelling studies on learning in the last several decades was done by Black and Wiliam (1998). In this study, the authors report that significant learning gains are made in an environment where students clearly understand the learning targets they are striving toward combined with giving formative feedback to help them self-evaluate their effectiveness toward reaching the desired target. To us, this means that what we expect our classroom learning environments to honor is self-organization. We expect that students be helped to understand the specific purpose for their work. We recognize that each learner is starting in a unique place and is uniquely wired, creating unique meaning from the material he or she interacts with, making synergistic connections between new ideas and past learning. We know that when students get formative feedback they are better able to achieve desired learning targets. We know that the teacher's role is to create the conditions for learning to emerge, not to just deliver the curriculum. The fact that our emerging educational practices are being influenced by the concepts of self-organization reflects a growing trend across many aspects of our lives.

TAKE A MOMENT

Think of the description of learning just presented. Visualize creating the conditions for this learning in an organization based in the command-and-control structure. Then visualize creating those conditions in an organization based in the self-organizing structure. As you envision these scenarios, which one best lends itself to this form of learning?

It is impossible to lead for innovation until one has a clear vision of what that entails. Through the remainder of the book, we will be giving you many more opportunities to envision yourself leading an innovative organization. We have brought forth four attributes of innovative systems:

(1) dissonance, (2) self-referencing, (3) amplification, and (4) engagement. These attributes, however, are not valued in the mind-sets that underlie traditional organizations. What we have described here is an organizing form that honors the attributes of innovation: self-organizing. We believe that learning more about this form of organization will enable leaders to envision the conditions that nurture innovation. The good news is that the concepts creating self-organization are naturally gaining more prominence as people around the world connect to one another and organize in ways not possible just a decade ago.

In the remainder of the book, we will keep expanding your understanding of self-organization. We will develop the four attributes in more detail in subsequent chapters. For now, what we want you to be thinking about is how your organization uses dissonance, how people connect to its purpose, how ideas grow and become noticed, how new practices replace old ones, and . . . how your organization might approach these differently.

SUMMARY

All educators today face great challenges in helping schools get better at the same time they strive to become different. Part of this challenge is to learn how to create innovation as well as improvement. In this chapter, we have outlined four attributes of innovative systems: (1) disturbance, (2) self-referencing, (3) amplification, and (4) engagement and how they support and assist leaders in moving into the complexities of innovation.

We also have revealed a dilemma that educators deal with as they address these challenges: The attributes of innovation are not attributes that are valued in the traditional organizational structure. This is because the underlying belief structures used to shape our organizations are based in classic Newtonian science. Newtonian science has envisioned the interactions of the world to be based on linear mathematics and mechanistic thinking. This has proven to be very useful thinking for hundreds of years, yet advances in modern science have proven that understandings of many phenomena require different views of how order is created. Replacing the mind-set of linearity, predictability, control, and stability are the importance of nonlinearity, disturbance, disequilibrium, and self-organization.

The principles of new science hold much potential for the development of organizations that are capable of adapting to changes in the external environment. Addressing the challenges facing education requires organizations that can change, adapt, and remain vital in relationship to the external environment—that can improve and innovate. Yet this is not easy work. At the same time educators are striving to accept the principles of self-organization, they are working in systems deeply rooted in command and control.

The ultimate challenge for educational leaders today as they seek to improve and innovate is to be in it but not of it. By this we mean, to work successfully in the world of command and control where measurement and predictability are driving forces but to not have their thinking be derived from this paradigm. We ask that leaders develop deeper understanding of the principles of self-organization and new science so that these ideals become a part of who they are. In this way, they can seek to stretch beyond current practice while still valuing the world where they are embedded.

SBK High School and the Attributes of Innovation

The Schools for the Future initiative undertaken by this system illustrates the focus of this chapter: the attributes of innovation. The first attribute is one of disturbance or being open to the experience even if it makes one feel uncomfortable. The 60-member group consisting of parents, school board members, community members, administrators, and teachers was uncomfortable facing the changes that are occurring globally. It was not easy to hear about losing a number of professional positions to other countries because the work can be done for less money. It was not easy to hear that the world dominance enjoyed by the United States might be in jeopardy. It was difficult to hear how young students use technology in their social experience to learn but have limited access in a school setting.

Members of the initiative extended these conversations back to their schools and districts. The dialogue that took place with school staffs and school boards at the local schools was referenced against the vision held for schooling. Using the second attribute of innovation, self-referencing, brought life to the meaning of their shared purpose. The disturbing information activated deep discussions about what it means to create relevant, engaging, and self-directed learning opportunities for all students. This system has begun to realize that broad conversations of this nature are a very important part of creating the conditions for adaptation.

Presently, the district is experiencing the third attribute of innovation: amplification of the meaning of emerging ideas and seeing important ones gain momentum. Dialogue is taking place with staff through conversations and with focus groups of students and focus groups of community members. As ideas have been clarified, shared understandings have strengthened commitment to the ideas.

The fourth attribute of innovation, engagement or the opportunity for new ideas to connect and compete with existing ideas, is just starting to take place. The system's leaders understand the importance of this step and are working to define the learning needs of the 21st-century learner. This will allow a playing field where ideas can compete against one another. Those that best meet these criteria will be implemented; those that do not will need to be diminished. In this way, they hope to provide a means for the best ideas to become part of the practice that defines the most effective teaching and learning techniques, structure of school day, use of time, and customized and innovative responses to learning needs.

SBK is a healthy system that exists on the edge of order and disorder. It has a strong identity, but is open to new information. This district's story is one that also exemplifies that a creative spark may come from anywhere. Who would have thought that a simple request to develop an approach to improve student writing with kindergarten through Grade 12 implications would result in a system's response to examine the learning needs of all learners?

TEAM CONVERSATION STARTERS

As a team, you may choose to explore the following questions:

- How does our organization respond when disturbance presents itself? Do we use it to our advantage or try to diminish it? How should it be?
- In our district, what do we use to reference our ideas and decisions against? What else might we use?
- How do ideas become noticed in our district? What can we do to encourage more of this, or what should we do differently?
- How do important ideas grow into widespread use in our district? Is this okay, or should we advocate for another way?
- Are there aspects of our organization that exhibit principles of self-organization? If so, what evidence do we have? If not, what can we do to encourage these principles?

Self-Assessment

Attributes of Innovation

Where am I in my ability to nurture the attributes of innovation? Mark which of these characteristics your leadership encourages and to what degree.

Disturbance		
Minimizing disturbances	♦——♦——♦——♦	Moving into disturbances
Looking for quick fixes	♦——♦——♦——♦	Exploring deeper issues
Self-Referencing		
Referencing needs of self	♦——♦——♦——♦	Referencing the big picture
Referencing current practices	♦——♦——♦——♦	Referencing preferred state
Amplification		
Keeping new ideas local	♦——♦——♦——♦	Ideas resonating systemically
People waiting for directives	♦——♦——♦——♦	People exploring
Engagement		
Department connections	♦——♦——♦——♦	Cross-function relationships
Work for compliance	♦——♦——♦——♦	Seek deeper meaning

Develop the Courage to Leap 4

The most important thing is this: to be ready at any moment to give up what you are for what you might become.

—Charles DuBois, literary critic

Innovative change is never accompanied by sufficient information and knowledge; it often requires acting wisely and prudently on the basis of minimum data, facts, and information.

—Dee Hock, founder of VISA

IN THIS CHAPTER

To truly lead, one needs to see beyond the immediate, ensure that a course to a desired future is charted, and help others move toward that future. The case we are making is that when educational leaders look beyond the immediate, they will see that the future they need to prepare students for is markedly different from the past. Educators will need to chart a course to the future that involves a new destination—one where students acquire new skills and capacities to compete in a globalized world. This book is not about where that destination is. It is about bringing awareness to the fact that once educators determine where that destination is, the journey to get there requires leaving many old ways behind so that new, more productive methods of teaching and learning can be implemented. It is the journey of innovation, and it is fraught with challenges.

It is a journey that starts with thinking about organizations and how they are led and managed. As we pointed out in the previous chapter, our organizational forms—and our thinking about leading them—have been based on the science of 300 years ago. In this view, predictability and control hold premiums. However, leadership based on predictability and control does not allow the space for ambiguity and uncertainty, which are foundational for innovative endeavors.

The dilemma for educational leaders is that they need to move their systems to new destinations and, at the same time, recognize that they are working in systems that want to get better at reaching old destinations. This is why we stated in the previous chapter that the ultimate challenge for educational leaders is to function in the world of command and control where measurement and predictability are driving forces but not to have their thinking be derived from it. To lead for innovation requires new expectations for leaders. One way to help understand what those expectations are is by visualizing innovation life cycles as an S-curve function.

INNOVATION LIFE CYCLES

The Sigmoid mathematical function is an S-shaped curve, often used to describe life cycles over time (Figure 4.1). The S-curve in Figure 4.1 represents the growth cycles of systems and ideas and can be thought of as a general learning curve. It has been used to describe the life cycle of many phenomena from embryo development, to learning to ride a bike, to product innovation, to professional careers, to technological advancements, to the rise and fall of nations. The nature of the growth cycle represented by the S-curve makes it well suited as a means to visualize the difference between leading for improvement and leading for innovation.

| Figure 4.1 | S-Curve Cycle |

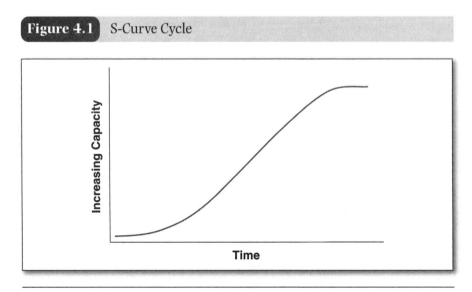

Everett Rogers (1995) connected the S-curve with innovation as early as his work in the 1960s. Rogers studied the phenomenon of innovation and the rate at which innovative ideas are diffused. He found that "when the number of individuals adopting a new idea is plotted on a cumulative frequency basis over time, the resulting distribution is an S-shaped curve" (p. 22–23).

The length, duration, and slope of this curve vary, but its overall shape metaphorically illustrates the challenges facing leaders as they work in systems needing both improvement and innovation. Leading for improvement is about riding the wave of an S-curve life cycle to get the most out of it. Leading for innovation is about leaping to a new S-curve wave at just the right time before the old wave runs out of energy.

For understanding the life cycle of practices in education, the S-curve framework provides a means for visualizing the introduction, growth, and maturation of ideas as shown in Figure 4.2. The dynamics of the S-curve are as follows. When an idea is first introduced, its assimilation is slow as people are learning to match its capabilities to unsolved problems. For example, the acceptance of computer processing power into the home was slow, as many experts at first saw few applications for home use. Once its potential applications were understood and embraced, its dissemination into homes rapidly accelerated.

Figure 4.2   S-Curve Life Cycle Stages

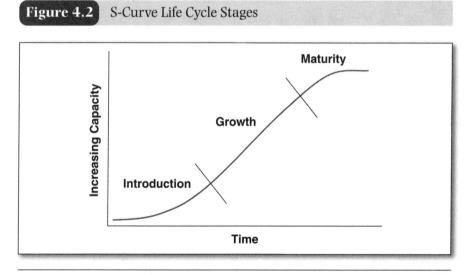

If the idea solves some problems that were not solved with the old practice, then it gains acceptance and its growth rate increases. Because of its success, the idea is applied more and more, eventually becoming the new operating practice, where it will be used to address new problems and new opportunities.

While the new idea is in the growth period, people are excited because it helps solve pressing problems. The growth stage is a stage well suited to improvement, where new applications and adjustments are made to the idea while remaining in the core of its current capacity. Yet no idea solves all the problems. Eventually, as the new idea becomes more widely accepted, it will be stretched beyond its original parameters facing problems it was not intended to solve.

At this stage, people often find it difficult to let go of the skills, concepts, and knowledge that led to its former success. The idea has reached a plateau. In this mature stage, people struggle to solve emerging problems with the now established practice. Inefficiency increases. Past confidence in the idea's ability to solve problems will wane as people begin to notice that the idea is not well suited to address emerging problems. In such cases, the usual response is to try to apply the new idea anyway, assuming it is the answer.

The Individuals with Disabilities Education Act (IDEA) legislation enacted by Congress in the 1970s has followed an S-curve cycle. This law provided public education to millions of children with disabilities who previously had been excluded from public schools. The legislation has been modified, amended, and improved many times over the years, most recently in 2004. Interpreting the law was awkward at first for educators. Once they began to understand its parameters, the thinking behind IDEA was increasingly applied to solve students' learning problems. IDEA reached the mature stage when populations of special education students grew beyond original intentions, as getting extra services through qualifying students for special education became a ready remedy for many situations.

TAKE A MOMENT

What new problems have come your way in the past year? Have you been trying to solve those problems by applying current proven practices? Has this process solved the new emerging problem? If so, in what ways? If not, why not?

Have new ideas emerged that based on current data look to be more effective in resolving your current problem? Are you and others receptive to embracing these new ideas? If not, what is hindering the embracement of new ideas?

At the mature stage, the idea is reaching the end of its shelf life. The law of diminishing returns takes over. The time and energy spent on improving this idea to address new challenges do not produce corresponding returns in productivity because the now mature idea is not *genetically coded* to solve the emerging problems. At this point, a new set of knowledge and skills is needed. A *new*, new idea must emerge to address the new challenges. This is the time to see the situation as an adaptive challenge rather than a technical problem. Getting the most out of an S-curve life cycle is improvement; leaping to a new one is innovation. What we are saying is that the logical, most effective means for continuous, healthy, adaptive organizational growth involves letting go of old practices as they reach the mature stage of their life cycle and embracing a fresh life cycle with a new idea as shown in Figure 4.3.

Figure 4.3   S-Curve Leap

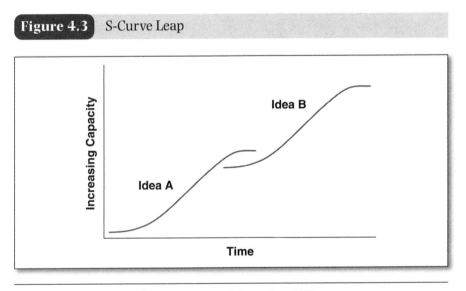

The dilemma for organizations at this stage is that the leap of letting go of old practices to accept a totally new one relies on making decisions with a minimal amount of information. This is not valued by mind-sets that seek predictability and control. This makes it scary to employees and counterintuitive to many leaders who are conditioned to value the attributes of command-and-control organizations. Making the leap is akin to letting go of the trapeze and flying to the waiting arms of the next trapeze artist—without the training to do so.

The leap from one S-curve life cycle to another is simple in concept. Yet in practice, it is extremely difficult for most organizations and the people in them. This is because the allure to keep applying the mature idea because it has proven itself to be effective is so strong—and the fear of leaping to an unproven idea is so disconcerting that people turn away from the need to change.

Lurking behind the virtues of innovation are two painful truths. First, innovation can be a pain in the neck for leaders—a nuisance, a disruption, an inconvenience, and even worse, a risk. Second, it is hard for leaders to predict or control innovation; the innovation process is messy rather than orderly. (Kanter, 2002, p. 77)

Avoiding the leap because of the potential to lose control or the fear of getting messy is a perilous choice. Continuing to look for answers within current practices when a leap to a new cycle is needed keeps an organization in stagnation, eventually leading to a loss of relevance and decline as shown in Figure 4.4.

> Only those most attuned to their organization's vision, structures, processes, hopes, and dreams know when it is time to let go of old ways and leap to new ones.

Figure 4.4   S-Curve Stagnation

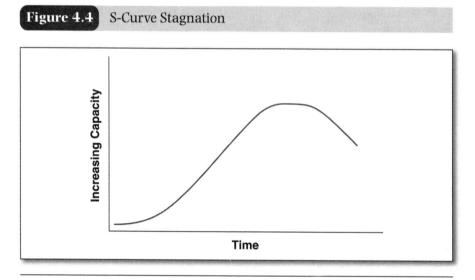

We believe that this leap from a mature growth cycle to a new life cycle is the essence of innovative leadership. Leadership is defined by the courage to use disturbances to see past the status quo and to evaluate where the organization is versus where it wants to be. Through that process, innovative leaders develop the resolve to look below the surface of their practice to the underlying mental models. They are not afraid to let the result of their reflection engage their mental models to see if some new, more potent understanding can come to the surface.

The rewards are organizational adaptation and rejuvenation. Yet the risks are high. Letting go of practices in an old life cycle and leaping to a new one often creates confusion, anxiety, and frustration—healthy for an organization in moderation but toxic if prolonged. Leaping too early in the growth cycle or too late is sure to create inefficiencies and declines in performance. Leaping to the wrong new idea is likely to have disastrous results as its consequence.

What leaders face today is a dilemma where hanging on to the status quo in times of rapidly changing external environments is certain to eventually lead to declining performance—and leaping to new ideas just for the sake of leaving the status quo is just as dangerous. There is no formula to determine when it's time to leap. Only those most attuned to their organization's vision, structures, processes, hopes, and dreams know when it is time to let go of old ways and leap to new ones. These times require that leaders honestly and wisely evaluate their organization's current performance and evaluate that against what the future requires.

These times require that leaders work with all involved to carefully examine assumptions and mental models to challenge and stretch visions of what is possible. And these times require that leaders help all involved project beyond self-interest to move through transitional times characterized by ambiguity and uncertainty to reach new levels of capacity. These times require leaders to apply new understandings of leadership. These times require leadership courage. This is true whether one is leading a classroom, school, district, or university.

TAKE A MOMENT

What mental models in your organization currently drive the direction and decision making in your district? How do those mental models support or hinder addressing what the future requires of your school or district?

THE HERO'S JOURNEY

Fortunately, the need to respond proactively to such leadership challenges is nothing new. Such responses have been seen as important for thousands of years. Author and scholar Joseph Campbell (1991) identified this as the hero's journey. He found the pattern of the hero's journey to be one consistently represented in the mythology and story of every culture across time. This journey has great relevance for understanding what it takes to lead for innovation, for it represents the characteristics needed to move from one S-curve life cycle to another.

Campbell (1991) identifies that the hero journey is one involving "departure, fulfillment, return" (p. 166). He has characterized this journey as the process where individuals leave their present condition (either by choice or by circumstance); go out into the unknown or the wilderness and acquire new capacity, understanding, or power; and then ultimately, return to share the new finding with others.

It is vital to emphasize here that we are not suggesting that what is needed for innovation is the "John Wayne," leader-as-hero archetype, where the leader carries the organization on his or her back. That is the antithesis of what is needed. What we are emphasizing here is the courageous journey of transformation—leaving one state of capacity to quest for a higher one.

> In order to found something new, one has to leave the old and go in quest of the seed idea, a germinal idea that will have the possibility of bringing forth that new thing. . . . You might say that the founder of a life—your life or mine, if we live our own lives, instead of imitating everybody else's life—comes from a quest as well. (Campbell, 1991, pp. 166–167)

Campbell's (1991) description of the hero's quest to bring forth something new matches what is required of leaders as they move from the understanding in an old S-curve life cycle to a new one. Making such a shift requires a departure from an established practice or belief. After the departure, one enters a period of uncertainty and reorientation that, once resolved, leads to new capacity. In story and myth, this is a time of trial and tribulation, where the hero confronts the dragon in the cave or successfully completes three challenges and then gains new power. In our individual lives and in organizations doubt, ambiguity, uncertainty, and rigidity take the place of the dragon in the cave. After going through the darkness of uncertainty and ambiguity, the new seed idea emerges and the organizational hero brings it back and helps people envision a better state by sharing his or her new insights. Following this, the organization begins a new S-curve life cycle.

DEVELOPING THE COURAGE TO INNOVATE

Unique to our current times is the recognition that the pace of change means that we cannot rely solely on our organization's formal leaders to take the hero's journey. Rather, it is important for leaders to create the conditions where heroes can emerge from anywhere within the organization. Today's organizations require leadership capable of creating a working environment where the "germinal idea that will have the possibility of bringing forth that new thing" (Campbell, 1991, p. 167) can come from anyone, anywhere in the organization—not just from the top of the organizational chart. This means establishing a culture that possesses the courage to innovate, and it begins by developing leadership courage throughout the organization. We define *leadership courage as possessing the ability to let go of past practice when necessary, to move into the void of uncertainty, to take adaptive action while at times having only minimal information, and to develop the trust that allows others to follow to the new destination.*

TAKE A MOMENT

Based on the previous content, discuss an example where leadership courage was evident in your organization. If you can't think of one, what factors were present that prevented leadership courage from taking place?

What Does a Culture of Innovation Look Like in Personal Practice?

So what does the courage to innovate look like in schools? The good news is that there are many kernels of innovative leadership we can perceive if we have the lenses with which to see them. Our hope is to make these behaviors more visible and connect them to the attributes of innovation so that they can overtly be nurtured and developed.

When working with student teachers or aspiring administrators our experience has been that we are often able to predict, in a short time, whether that person will be effective. What we notice first is that those who turn out to be highly effective educators show signs early on of having a strong sense of purpose and identity while being reflective and malleable. These individuals come to the profession believing they can make a difference. They identify with broad values, ideals, and beliefs, such as "all children can learn," and they believe that "children will learn with me," or "this school will be great with me leading it."

Although most new teachers and administrators come with this idealism, those that develop into our best educators have another attribute that compliments their idealism. These individuals also have a certain sense of humility. They recognize that they are a piece of a larger whole and that to achieve their destiny with that larger whole of valued educators they have much to learn—and they are open to that learning. Their balance of idealism and humility focuses their learning on bringing their beliefs to life—"I know I can make a difference for kids. I don't know how to handle every situation yet, but I will eventually. I will refine my skills and get better and better." As Ken Blanchard and Norman Vincent Peal (quoted in Blanchard, 2007) state so simply, "People with humility don't think less of themselves, they just think of themselves less" (p. 60).

For other new teachers and administrators who do not view themselves as part of something larger, the degree of humility is not as strong. As they reference their development against their beliefs, their ego steps in to protect them from the professional discomfort of not having completely actualizing their beliefs. This turns their internal dialogue into, "I know I can make a difference. I haven't for this child. There must be something wrong with this child." These individuals are more likely to define their practice around only their successes. Those that develop into great teachers/administrators go beyond that and define their practice by what they learn after a child doesn't succeed or something does not produce the expected result. What we suggest is that these individuals are demonstrating the first two attributes of innovative systems, while the other new teachers and administrators do not. They are choosing to be disturbed by what's not working and are creating the motivation to move into that experience by referencing their beliefs and realizing that they are not there, *yet*.

> People with humility don't think less of themselves, they just think of themselves less.
>
> —Ken Blanchard and Norman Vincent Peale (quoted in Blanchard, 2007, p. 60)

What these good teachers and administrators do is create a hunger for learning by moving back and forth with their perspective—from the big picture to the personal/practical and back to the big picture again. They start from a perspective where they relate to and assimilate broad theory or beliefs. Their assimilated beliefs or vision shape what they perceive in their classrooms or schools. Then, they break down that theory and belief into personal meaning based on their reality. After this, they translate their personal meaning back to a refined and more clearly defined set of beliefs, values, or a vision, and the cycle begins over again with new situations. These people are hungry to be reconnected to their deeper selves and to those whom they serve.

This perspective is very comparable to the third and fourth attributes of innovation: amplification and engagement. Certain beliefs resonate and are amplified by what they see students doing in their classrooms—"All students can learn. This one did not, but she did when I did it another way last week. I wonder if I can adjust what I'm doing now to make it like what we did last week." For administrators this internal dialogue might be, "People don't seem to be on board with our current initiative, yet. I know that people need to create personal meaning for the changes they experience. Maybe what I've done to engage them in the past isn't working for this initiative, but they do seem interested in having time to collaborate. Maybe I can find ways to get them collaborating about the meaning of the new initiative."

The engagement stage of the innovative attributes is present when the teacher's mental model of what works is engaged and modified— "The adjustments I made for that student worked so well that I think I should modify the way I teach that concept to all my students." Likewise, for the administrator, the mental model of what works is challenged and modified: "I think my mental model of control has caused me to be too narrow in how I've engaged the staff in working together. When I set the reference points and let them work within that, they really came up with some great ideas. I'm going to take this to heart as we move forward with our new initiative."

What we notice in effective educators is that these individuals inherently value the need for disturbance to cause some form of creative tension between where they are and where they want to be. They tend to create energy for change by referencing this tension against their beliefs to help focus and sharpen their beliefs. Through that reflective process, they develop the resolve to look below the surface of their practice to the underlying mental models. They are not afraid to let the result of their reflection engage their mental models to see if some new, more potent understanding can come to the surface. In their practice, they instinctively use the four attributes of innovative systems: (1) choosing to be disturbed, (2) self-referencing, (3) amplification, and (4) engagement. These individuals develop intuitively the personal practices that we hope to develop consciously in others.

What Does a Culture of Innovation Look Like in Schools?

We can point to individual teacher and administrator attributes and say that they correspond to the attributes of innovative systems; however, it is much harder to do the same on a school or district level. Although we find some examples, such as those described in Chapter 2, it is not nearly as many as we would like. Kanter (2002) observes that it is "easier for leaders to praise innovation in theory than to support it in practice" (p. 77).

We find that on a personal, introspective level many effective educators value and intuitively use the attributes of innovation. However, they are far less likely to recognize their value and use these attributes on a broader systemic level. We think that this is because there is a big difference between going through this process on a personal, introspective level and doing so as part of a schoolwide or communitywide change initiative.

A definite feeling of messiness and discomforting ambiguity characterize the four attributes of innovation when people functioning in command-and-control organizations first encounter them because they fly in the face of predictability and control. Both of which are highly valued by organizations and many individuals associated with them. The messiness and ambiguity are much easier to manage on a personal, introspective level than they are when faced by an entire school community. It is one thing to value these attributes on your own; it is another thing to ask others to value them as a group. This is especially true when the dominating expectation of leaders is to create certainty and to protect us from messes and discomfort.

> When this leap comes from desperation, the success rate is low.

What we find is that although this leap to a new S-curve life cycle is something not understood or valued in most organizations, it can happen—but often not willfully. It is more likely to happen in situations where failure has taken a system out of equilibrium and created a sense of desperation or urgency than it is in situations where systems are successful as measured by past benchmarks of success. When this leap comes from desperation, the success rate is low. When it does happen willfully, it is because these systems have a culture that tolerates the creative tension created by discordant information matched against a strong identity or purpose. Their culture seeks to amplify the meaning created by solving learning problems with new techniques and engaging what is learned in the process against existing practice. In a culture such as this, the leap is more likely to be viewed as a natural process and is not as likely to be feared.

We believe the well-being of our nation's system of education depends on developing more leaders with the capabilities of shaping school cultures that foster innovation. To do that, the importance of these private, personal, introspective, reflective practices used by effective teachers and administrators and their impact and importance for leading our schools into the challenges of the future need to be brought out into the light of day for all to assimilate.

It is our intent in Part II, Essential Leadership Practices, to help leaders create organizational cultures that are more likely to appreciate the leap than to fear it. Foundational to those practices is the willingness for leaders to develop a *well-traveled* inner path to the core of their leadership beliefs and motivation. To assist in developing this path, the next chapter is devoted to a concept we call the courageous conversation. The courageous conversation opens the door for the development of leadership practices that form the foundation of an innovative organization. Chapters 6 through 9 reference the attributes of innovation as part of the framework used for developing four essential leadership practices: (1) *embrace dissonance,* (2) *create context,* (3) *change your field of perception,* and (3) *let ideas collide.* Resource B, at the end of the book, brings these all together to create the essential leadership actions to help you on your journey to innovative leadership.

SUMMARY

The S-curve provides a means for visualizing the life cycle of ideas. With this model, we are better able to discuss the tasks leaders face as they help their organizations both improve and innovate. Improvement involves making the most out of a present S-curve life cycle while innovation requires a leap to a new S-curve life cycle. Although it is simple to describe the theory behind the S-curve life cycle, in practice the leap to a new S-curve is difficult for leaders. This is because it can be risky, messy, and perilous, particularly when people in organizations want to stay with the status quo rather than suffer the pain of losing their comfort with the old way.

Innovation involves a leap to a new S-curve—and this requires leadership courage. Leaders can draw confidence from the fact that calling on this courage is not a new concept, rather one that has been required throughout history. Campbell (1991) defines accessing this courage as the hero's journey. It is how ordinary people, on a personal as well as public level, develop higher capacities. It is helpful for leaders to navigate the stages of this journey, as they help their organizations innovate. We believe that the courage to innovate using the attributes of innovation closely parallels the hero's journey.

It is also important to recognize that organizations benefit when their leaders create conditions that encourage everyone in the organization to access the hero's journey. This is because in today's world the fast pace of change requires that organizations adapt quickly to changes in their environment. For this to occur, organizations have to create cultures where the seed idea for the next S-curve life cycle can come from anyone, anywhere in the organization—not just from the top of the organization.

We find that on a personal, introspective level many educators intuitively use the four innovation attributes. Yet, it is much more difficult to find evidence of their use on a larger scale at a school or district level. By making the stages of this process more visible, and by describing their use on systemic levels, we hope that on a widespread level people will move these practices from an intuitive to a conscious level. The remainder of the book is dedicated to that end.

SBK High School: Knowing When to Leap to a New S-Curve

The districts illustrated in this story have a history of improving learning for students and staff to increase student achievement. Over the last several years, there has been an emphasis on improving reading for all students.

Although standardized scores initially increased, they subsequently leveled off. Recently, the high school introduced a technology-driven approach to address the issue of improving reading and comprehension. A short time ago, the high school district was notified that it had not met Adequate Yearly Progress (AYP) according to the No Child Left Behind legislation for students with disabilities in the area of reading.

In response, several new ideas were identified to improve reading for students with disabilities, including the use of technology. It is anticipated that growth will occur and standardized test scores will go up. This is an effort to improve. The schools leaders also recognize that they will need to anticipate when the ideas reach maturation and a leap to new techniques will need to take place. They look for new opportunities constantly because they know that what impacts learning for students with disabilities may come from another area—and what impacts learning for students with disabilities may positively elevate the learning of all students.

Leaders at SBK High School and its feeder districts continue to work at reaching the goals set forth in the No Child Left Behind legislation; at the same time, through, their Schools of the Future initiative, they are examining learning needed for the 21st-century learner. Leaders in this initiative are discussing how they will know when it is time to stop improving a current practice, let go, and encourage the emergence of new ideas, thus, facilitating a leap to the next S-curve life cycle.

TEAM CONVERSATION STARTERS

As a team, you may choose to explore the following questions:

- What compelling issues or problems are currently facing your district or school? Where are these issues on the S-curve life cycle?
- Is your district or school viewing these as a technical problem or as an adaptive challenge?
- What issues or problems do you feel demand an innovative approach and why?
- What would it take to create the capacity for your district or school to leap to a new S-curve life cycle to bring these innovative approaches into practice?
- What do you feel are the personal strengths needed to lead others into innovation?
- With those personal strengths, how can your team support yourselves and others during the possible discomfort of innovation?

Self-Assessment

Develop the Courage to Leap

Use this self-assessment to help start a process of personal reflection that allows you to assess your willingness to take the leap to a new S-curve life cycle—your leadership courage. Mark on the continuum where you see your leadership right now. After completing the self-assessment, find a quiet moment to replay your last few days. What evidence can you uncover in your reflection to support your assessment? I find comfort with the following:

The status quo	♦——♦——♦——♦	Seeing past the status quo
Well-formed ideas	♦——♦——♦——♦	Ambiguous ideas
Focusing on the present	♦——♦——♦——♦	Focusing on the future
Keeping the peace	♦——♦——♦——♦	Stirring the pot
Procedure and consistency	♦——♦——♦——♦	Purpose and flexibility
Playing close to the vest	♦——♦——♦——♦	Being open and taking risks
Someone leading the way	♦——♦——♦——♦	Leading the way
Following the rules	♦——♦——♦——♦	Discovering new rules

Hold Courageous Conversations   **5**

Often, in common parlance, the words creativity and innovation are used interchangeably. They shouldn't be, because while creativity implies coming up with ideas, it's the 'bringing ideas to life' . . . that makes innovation the distinct undertaking it is.

—R. Tucker, author and consultant

The most important conversation to have in the process of transformation is with oneself. The willingness to stare down fears, challenge limiting mental models, and argue with existing assumptions is requisite to real change. And yes, it takes courage, but it creates possibility.

—Nancy Stanford Blair, professor and author
(personal correspondence, February 2009)

IN THIS CHAPTER

Leadership that fosters improvement and innovation is not only about developing new understandings, but it is also very much about having the courage to commit to bringing those understandings into practice. As was presented in Chapter 4, the courage to bring innovative ideas into practice involves leaping to a new S-curve life cycle. The attributes of innovation, *choosing to be disturbed, self-referencing, amplification, and engagement,* help create the organizational conditions where the leap is less fearful, yet walking the path of the hero's journey is still required.

Building leadership capacity at this level involves an inner journey. The path of that journey starts with one's orientation to change. One's orientation to change is the focus of this chapter. An individual's change orientation either opens one to adaptation and innovation or limits one's ability to move beyond the status quo. According to John Maxwell (2003), "Nothing is more difficult to accomplish than changing our outward actions without changing our inward feelings" (p. 35).

As a means for starting an inner journey, this chapter introduces the concept of courageous conversations. Courageous conversations are those inner dialogues that bring forth the courage and character necessary to move into disturbances to create the conditions for innovation, opposed to seeing disturbances as threats and trying to make them go away.

PERSONAL ORIENTATION TO CHANGE

Whether the focus is improvement or innovation, leaders are dealing with change. Many authors have analyzed the topic, giving leaders sound theories for what is involved in change and giving strategies for using its nuances to their advantage. It is not our intent to add new theories to the body of knowledge regarding change. We accept the premise of many who write about transformative change and organizations (Fullan, 2008; Marshall, 2006; Senge, Scharmer, Jaworski, & Flowers, 2004; Wheatley, 1997, 1999a, 1999b, 2005, 2006, 2007) who adapt a view from recent science, which shifts the dynamics of change from a mechanistic metaphor to a dynamic, adaptive, and living, whole-system metaphor. These authors inform us that dynamic systems (which schools are) are changing over time and that disorder, instability, disequilibrium, and nonlinear relationships are elements that living systems use to adapt. We believe that these also describe the conditions conducive to organizational innovation. As authors, we particularly appreciate the work of Pascale, Millemann, and Gioja (2000). They summarize four important change principles of living systems as follows:

1. *Equilibrium* is a precursor to *death.* When a living system is in a state of equilibrium, it is less responsive to changes occurring around it. This places it at maximum risk.

2. In the face of threat, or when galvanized by a compelling opportunity, living systems move toward the *edge of chaos.* This condition evokes higher levels of mutation and experimentation, and fresh new solutions are more likely to be found.

3. When this excitation takes place, the components of living systems *self-organize* and new forms and repertoires *emerge* from the turmoil.

4. Living systems cannot be *directed* along a linear path. Unforeseen consequences are inevitable. The challenge is to *disturb* them in a manner that approximates the desired outcome. (p. 6)

Equilibrium as a precursor to death, the edge of chaos as the place where new solutions are found, self-organizing and emergent behavior, disturbing instead of directing—these themes may be becoming more familiar to you now —if not more comfortable. And they may challenge your mental model of change.

Innovation occurs in leaps in response to adaptive challenges. It involves the type of change where new ways are learned and, heretofore, unknown ideas and behaviors emerge. Change of this type is not incremental; it is transformative and adaptive. The natural world teaches us about this form of change. It teaches that transformative change involves more volatility than we may be used to, particularly when old science supports the importance of equilibrium and stability. Adaptive change happens at the edge of chaos.

Key Elements of Change

We define the key elements of adaptive change as disturbance, identity, information, and order. Adaptive change in natural systems starts with a *disturbance.* The disturbance brings something unfamiliar to the system. The system references this unfamiliarity against its *identity*—its sense of self—to determine its importance and meaning. In this process of determining meaning, new *information* is generated. The new information is circulated through the networks of individual entities—be that cells in a body or members of a herd. Each entity interprets the new information and modifies its meaning. If the collective meaning grows to a point that the system must respond, then its existing *order* is engaged. If the system cannot respond in its present structure, then it must reorder itself—this means it must allow its present order to break apart so that a new order can form.

Innovation is born in the conditions closer to the end of the change spectrum defined by these four elements than it is at the end of the spectrum offering analysis, measurement, and prescriptive action steps. You may not be able to articulate in detail the scientific concepts behind the four change elements. Yet we hope that, at this point, some stirring is activated within you. We hope that these principles are reaching places deep inside of you— that they are beginning to resonate with undernourished beliefs lying dormant in your soul. Developing leadership practices that support innovation means that you may need to uncover, and potentially replace, the deep-seated beliefs and mental models that presently drive your leadership.

TAKE A MOMENT

How do these principles align with your beliefs about creating change? Could the discord you may be feeling be a signal that this is where your internal change needs to begin?

Courageous Conversations

Understanding your mental models and their orientation to change will go a long way in helping you develop as a leader of innovation. As leaders, most of our training regarding change has been about planning and engineering it. Yet the type of change we just described is where S-curve leaps and innovative change takes place.

In this book, we are encouraging you to think differently about leadership. We are asking you to add to your leadership repertoire concepts such as disequilibrium, ambiguity, perturbations, nonlinear relationships, and reordering. Doing so may require deep shifts from current mental models. Such shifts require transitions, not just

> A courageous conversation may make you weep, jump for joy, tumble with emotions, and cry for help.

changes in knowledge. Author William Bridges (1991) identifies transitions as "the psychological process people go through to come to terms with the new situation" (p. 3). To help provide the space where you can examine your mental models of change, innovation, and leadership so that you can transition to new mental models, we are providing you with a practice we refer to as a courageous conversation.

The term *courageous conversation* is used in many contexts. Most prominently, it is used in the work of Singleton and Linton (2006) as a strategy to encourage educators to engage in discussions about how to deinstitutionalize racism and improve achievement. We use the term differently in our thinking about moving into dissonance to bring about deep, life-altering change. Pauli introduced our team to the term years ago, as she described the internal dialogue she had used many times when she faced life-altering situations. It is in this context—a tough, clarifying internal dialogue—that we use the term.

A *courageous conversation is an internal dialogue with your heart and mind that influences your spirit and your life.* The most important courageous conversation is the one where you gather all of your courage to have a conversation with yourself, by yourself, over time. Actually, until you learn to have one with yourself, you will not be able to have one with others. It is a deeply reflective journey of self-discovery that unveils and exposes the good, the bad, and the hidden wholeness within one's soul. This conversation introduces you to yourself, with all your strengths and perceived limitations, exposing yourself at a very intimate level, and it usually occurs when you are in a state of disequilibrium, a state brought on as you come to terms with some aspect of change.

Such a conversation is one that you have to set aside time for, not one that you tuck into the brief gaps and quick spaces of your busy life. You can hold one when you are on a walk, when you are sitting quietly on your deck, while you are curled up on your couch, or even when you are soaking in the tub. The aloneness, the quietness, the stillness, the tranquility of the place you select to have your ongoing conversation provides the ambiance for intimate reflection and deep glimpses into your heart and soul. It is a period to listen; to observe; and to expose your innermost feelings, thoughts, and desires; it is a time when you shut down the "doer" and take the time to be. A courageous conversation may make you weep, jump for joy, tumble with emotions, and cry for help, all with the hope of confronting the dissonance that struggles and squirms within you. This is because it is privately moving you to the place where new capacities are found—the edge of chaos.

It is not a one-time dialogue but a conversation that ruminates and rumbles, ebbs, and flows within your heart and mind off and on for days, weeks, or even months until the "aha" moments and intimate reflections expose you to a path you may have otherwise not taken. It is one filled with a renewed consciousness and sense of self along with the hope, promise and courage to allow you to move into another realm of your life. A courageous conversation is stimulated when you ask yourself the following:

- Am I engaged in an internal or external struggle?
- What is the struggle and how badly do I want to move into uncertainty to resolve it?
- Do I want to embrace the struggle, pretend it doesn't exist, or make it go away quickly?
- Am I courageous enough to listen to my inner being even when I discover things I don't want to hear?

Courageous conversations can take more than one path depending on the readiness and openness of the person. The readiness and openness of the person also influence the depth of reflection, fueling the courageous conversation. A controlled courageous conversation can be likened to improving yourself by desiring to be a better person than you are today. This conversation happens when you are open to qualms and uncertainties, but you want your internal and external environments to remain stable, predictable, and in your control. You are more interested in consistency and harmony than in resolving issues at a deeper, more intense dynamic level. This type of courageous conversation usually does not involve a shift in mental models.

SUE'S STORY

After months of reflection and courageous conversations, Sue, a kindergarten through Grade 5 special education teacher for 10 years, decided to leave her role and take a position as a second-grade teacher in the same school. Her dilemma was whether she should stay in her position as an advocate for her students or do what was ultimately best for her mental health and well-being. Eventually, her decision was made based on her inability to craft a quality child-centered relationship with several of her students' teachers who had different philosophies about students with special needs. She decided it was simply easier for her to walk away from the issues with these teachers and take a classroom position at a grade level with colleagues who shared her student-centered philosophy. Her decision was grounded in a more controlled conversation that allowed her to focus on what was best for her rather than dealing with the broader conflicting philosophical issues that frame special education.

Or you can take the courageous conversation to a much deeper, more profound path of change. To have a profound impact, you must have a desire to seek out and understand new realities, embrace dissonance, and revel in ambiguous behaviors that may take you to a place you may not even know exists. In this conversation, you are willing to see your external environment as unpredictable, fluctuating, and uncertain, all with the intent of profoundly altering both your internal and external environments.

JOHN'S STORY

John was a highly successful superintendent in an affluent school district when he decided that something was missing in his life. After long, agonizing conversations with himself for almost a year, he decided to follow his heart and take a principalship in a poverty-stricken, struggling district. This would allow him to be of service to others and to have more contact with students and staff rather than staying in a position that provided him with prominence, power, and authority—to say nothing of the benefits that his income added to his family's lifestyle. His original courageous conversations did not include exposing his uncertainties to his wife and children because he feared they would see his decision to leave his position as a step down.

> A courageous conversation is the path that starts one on a personal hero's journey to where new mental models change the way one views the world.

It wasn't until he resolved the issue with his head and heart that he revealed his thoughts to his family. Much to his surprise, they supported his decision and helped ease his transition from one position to another in a new district that was in desperate need of a highly qualified leader. Even though he had to move his family and change positions, he has never been happier. He moved back to his core purpose in life and recreated the vision that was always in his heart. His school, staff, and students have achieved many local, state, and national awards and recognitions, which constantly reinforce his decision to move into new possibilities and a more joyful life.

You may have noticed that in his courageous conversation John followed the path of the hero's journey:

Departure—he chose to let his unhappiness move him out of his comfort zone.

Fulfillment—he let his colliding ideas and reflections lead him to a place of inner peace and contentment where his idea of what he needed to do became his mission.

Return—he brought his idea to his family and found a place to connect his work and his purpose.

A courageous conversation is the path that starts one on a personal hero's journey to where new mental models change the way one views the world. At their essence, the deepest courageous conversations involve an internal dialogue that results from contrasting apparently opposed perspectives. In our usual thought processes, we tend to weigh one perception over another referenced against our existing beliefs: Should I choose Option 1 or 2 as an intervention option for this struggling learner? Should I purchase Car A or Car B based on my financial needs and the reviews I have read?

In a courageous conversation, perceptions are not weighed one over another—they are collided against each other. It is as if the ideas are attempting to be forced together creating a type of fusion. Rather than examining for differences, the ideas are first held together as part of the same whole, forcing the individual to consider the merits of both, not one over the other. In doing so, what tends to happen is that the referenced belief is seen in new light—not as which idea best suits this belief but as what does the relationship of these elements say about my belief. This shift causes one to evaluate his or her perception of, and relationship to, that belief. John's internal conversations became a deep courageous conversation when he collided his perceptions of job and role into a unified whole, so it caused him to examine his belief about professional purpose and fulfillment.

Courageous conversations start when ideas are held together trying to understand what binds them. This is when seeing opposing elements as part of the same whole, rather than seeing them in a dichotomy, is most useful. Once this is done, the mind shifts to seeking new patterns of connections rather than fitting ideas to existing patterns. For example, think about the ever-present debate about how to represent student learning through grading and report cards—an instrument designed to give feedback to parents. Should report cards follow the traditional A, B, C form or should they be directly linked to course standards, or should they be narrative in nature? Is the debate about report cards worth it? Should we just continue to use outdated reporting just to appease naysayers who say, "It was good enough for me; it's good enough for my kids." Think of how different our thinking is when we consider parents, students, and community all as users of student performance data. Thinking of all as users causes us to ask questions about the purpose of feedback and its relationship to student learning, rather than merely seeking the best method for informing parents.

Innovation is based in a different mental model than improvement. Unless one shifts to mental models where disturbance, disequilibrium, ambiguity, disorder, and challenging existing practice have a meaningful place, then innovation will be implemented through mental models that value stability, predictability, linearity, and control. It just won't work. Courageous conversations are a means to go on a personal journey where your mental models can be examined and altered, if necessary, so that innovation can be embraced. The deeper one is able to take a courageous conversation, the better able he or she is to make the adjustments to the shifts in understanding required by a leap to a new S-curve—one where innovation becomes a part of the leadership repertoire along with improvement.

To help you become more comfortable with the concepts associated with this shift to incorporating innovative leadership, we have linked the four change elements we have identified in this chapter to the four attributes of innovation presented in Chapter 3. This relationship is shown in Figure 5.1.

Figure 5.1 Attributes of Innovation

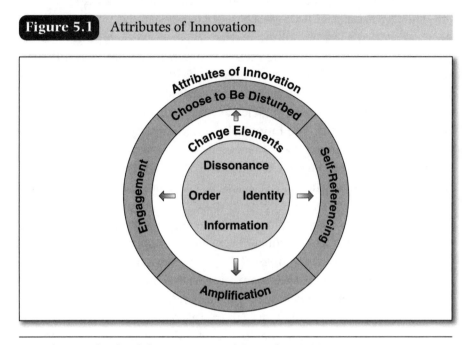

Copyright © Davidovich, Nikolay, Laugerman, and Commodore, 2009.

TAKE A MOMENT

Reflect on a time or situation that triggered a courageous conversation. Why did that particular time or place allow you to be more open with yourself? What resulted from that conversation? What is creating personal dissonance in your life right now? Should you have a courageous conversation now? If not, why not?

THE POWER OF PARADOXES

When we describe courageous conversations, we speak of the importance of holding ideas together, seeing them as part of the same whole rather than contrasting them. Doing so creates constructive paradoxes. Paradoxes are ideas that seem contradictory but, in reality, work together to define a larger whole. School leaders find no shortage of paradoxes as they go about their day: meet the challenges of tomorrow without challenging the status quo, bring all students to common standards of performance while you individualize your approach, provide structure and rigor while creating freedom, operate in organizations based in control and compliance while asking people to bring forth out-of-the-box solutions to problems.

Author Jim Collins (2005) has brought to public attention the concepts necessary for moving organizations from *good to great*. He states, "Great organizations keep clear the difference between their core values (which never change) and operating strategies and cultural practices (which endlessly adapt to a changing world)" (p. 35). This statement summarizes the ultimate paradox that educational leaders face as they attempt to help their school systems improve and innovate—to never change at the same time they are endlessly adapting.

Working with paradoxes forces us to see these apparent contradictions as part of the same whole. They allow us the chance to understand the relationship and connections between these concepts in a new light—not as contradictions but as complimentary weavings of the same tapestry.

In large part, deep courageous conversations are based around the recognition of a situation as a paradox. Like John, someone engaged in a deep courageous conversation holds elements together in a whole relationship that at first glance may appear to be opposed and competing. John struggled with following his head or his heart. His courageous conversation was driven by holding these elements together instead of trying to decide which one was right. In doing so, he journeyed to a place where a richer relationship to his beliefs could be revealed. In that place, amid the chaos, a calm focus is often found as one connects with a renewed commitment to purpose.

Courageous Conversations, Paradoxes, and the Internal Leadership Dialogue

John's courageous conversation revealed his inherent understanding of the power of an inner dialogue in leading one to new capacities, an understanding that is not unique to him. The stages of his courageous conversations reflect a common approach used by effective school leaders. Many of the effective leaders we work with express an inherent understanding that dissonance or discomfort starts the movement toward developing new capacities. They use their experience with dissonance to look past the stages of discomfort, trusting that they and their organizations will get to the other side. In the early stages of the process, these leaders usually acknowledge that their first efforts might be to keep things steady or that they may want a disturbance to go away. However, as the circumstances progress, they are able to recognize the opportunity being presented, and they, consequently, open themselves to the process.

These leaders resist applying a quick fix to a situation. Instead, they look for an opportunity to move into dissonance—they perceive it to be an opportunity to create momentum to move beyond the status quo.

The next question one might ask is how do leaders know when it is time to move into dissonance and when it is not? Our experiences and work with these leaders reveals that they tend to create the context to reference possibilities against before they engage their organizations in the process of change. This dynamic involves the use of exploring the dissonance created by apparent paradoxes. For example, they inherently understand that transformative change comes after a system is disturbed out of a state of equilibrium, yet at the same time, they value the system's desire for stability. Constantly aware of not being too far to one extreme or the other, the drive for balance is used to answer the inner question, what is the right thing to do?

In essence, these leaders use the paradoxes they perceive to create an inner conflict, which clarifies their understanding and resolve before they introduce such a conflict into the system as a whole. Their tendency is to bring together opposing perspectives on an issue with the intention of changing their perception of the issues.

Finally, just as in the return stage of Campbell's (1991) hero journey, these leaders take this new understanding and engage others in the change at hand. They reframe their understanding so that it relates to the world of those they serve. By letting ideas collide internally first, they better understand and account for the struggles that are inherent in the change process. In this way, these leaders are able to put themselves on the line for what is vital yet, perhaps, difficult—and help others do so as well.

From exploring the inner reflection and courageous conversations of effective leaders as they deal with difficult challenges, we have found that they use practices that intuitively parallel the change elements found in nature. They use these practices to make the inner adjustments required by the changes they face before bringing them to their organizations. Their practices can be summarized as follows:

- First, they move into dissonance instead of trying to make it go away.
- Second, they create a context to reference possibilities against before they engage in the process of change.
- Third, they change their field of perception of the events.
- Fourth, they let ideas collide so that deeper, richer understanding can emerge.

We bring to you the experience of a courageous conversation as an important technique for developing innovative leadership because it opens one to the inner hero's journey that builds the courage to not only change but also to transition to a new state. Also, it is presented to you because inherent in it is four leadership practices used by effective leaders that are essential for innovation: (1) embrace dissonance, (2) create context, (3) change your field of perception, and (4) let ideas collide. The relationship of these four practices to the change elements and innovative attributes is shown in Figure 5.2 and will be developed in more detail in the remaining chapters.

Figure 5.2   Essential Leadership Practices

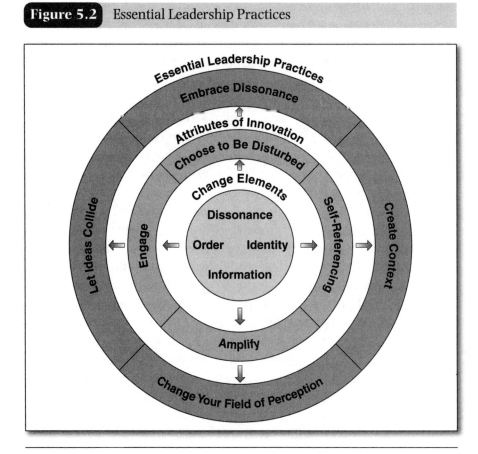

SUMMARY

Innovation does not involve the type of change that occurs in incremental steps. It comes about in leaps—leaps to new ways and new S-curves. This type of change is preceded by ambiguity, dissonance, disequilibrium, and breaking down of old order. It requires a different kind of leadership than improvement, and it is derived from a different mental model of change. To become a leader of innovation, one must examine practices at a level where mental models can shift to accommodate new understandings. To assist in that regard, we have introduced you to the concept of a courageous conversation—a deep internal dialogue that allows one to examine his or her beliefs, values, and mental models. Courageous conversations can be fueled by paradoxes. Paradoxes are seemingly contradictory ideas that are held together by examining them as part of the same whole. By seeing the situations around them in paradoxes, leaders are better able to engage in the internal dialogues that reveal mental models and allow for shifts in practice, a necessary mind-set for leaders of innovation.

Paradoxes are foundational for courageous conversations. And they are foundational for organizational mind-sets that balance improvement and innovation. Using this method allows leaders an inner mental rehearsal that strengthens resolve and prepares them for the challenges of moving an organization beyond its comfort zone to a new life cycle. Also, when leaders can help people examine problems as paradoxes, the mind works to make new connections to understand the whole created by apparently opposed ideas. These new connections form the seeds for innovation. Structuring conversations for improving student learning around paradoxes is an effective means for creating courageous conversations that help schools move beyond improvement to innovation. When we structure problem solving as the search for the right answer, no such connections are made. Courageous conversations will be foundational for developing the *how to* in the remaining chapters.

SBK High School: Holding Courageous Conversations

Leaders in the story of SBK High School engaged in courageous conversations individually and collectively in preparing to move into the Schools for the Future initiative. After much effort, the vision that was adopted was simple and meaningful to all districts. The next step was moving forward to obtain approval for eight school boards to proceed. It took courage and character on the part of leaders to move into the disturbance created by colliding ideas—and many individual courageous conversations were held to access deeply held beliefs and mental models. Although it was difficult, leaders recognized it as a necessary step to fostering innovation.

Leaders continue to have internal and external conversations as they seek to understand new realities and deal with ambiguities. The systems are being disturbed, and it would be very easy for the leaders to fall back on old beliefs about the importance of maintaining stability. Encouraging opportunity for rich dialogue when people expect leaders to provide answers takes courage. These leaders are able to muster that courage as they hold internal courageous conversations fueled by the paradox identified by Jim Collins (2005): envisioning what it means to help their systems never change while they endlessly adapt.

TEAM CONVERSATION STARTERS

As a team, explore the following questions:

- As an organization, do we view dissonance as a foe or an ally? Why or why not?
- Is our organization currently committed to only stability and control, or are we willing to move toward an environment of uncertainty and messiness that surrounds that leap from one S-curve to another?
- What issues must we address right now? What courageous conversations must we have with ourselves and others?
- What paradoxes surround our decision making and will hover over us as we move forward? How can we frame them so that they encourage courageous conversations?

Self-Assessment

Hold Courageous Conversations

We are at the midpoint of this book. That makes it a good time to reflect on how your thinking has evolved from the start. Take some time now to complete the self-assessment below. It is the same one that you completed at the end of Chapter 1—with one notable exception: The word "would" has been substituted for the original word "do" in all of the questions. After completing it, look back to your original work. How does it compare? What does it say about your thinking? It is okay if the comparison starts you on a courageous conversation—enjoy the inner dialogue.

How would you prefer to create change in your work environment?	Incrementally ◆—◆—◆—◆—◆—◆	In leaps
How would like to react to disturbances to the status quo?	Minimize them ◆—◆—◆—◆—◆—◆	Amplify them
What would you like to provide your teams as they go about their work?	Structure ◆—◆—◆—◆—◆—◆	Freedom
What kind of instruction would you like to offer to improve student learning?	Standardized ◆—◆—◆—◆—◆—◆	Customized
What would most help people know what is important in your organization?	Directives ◆—◆—◆—◆—◆—◆	Relationships
How would you prefer information to move through your organization?	Controlled ◆—◆—◆—◆—◆—◆	Free flowing
What type of problem solving would you like to use to analyze data?	Convergent ◆—◆—◆—◆—◆—◆	Divergent

Part II

Essential Leadership Practices

Four essential leadership practices, (1) *embrace dissonance,* (2) *create context,* (3) *change your field of perception,* and (4) *let ideas collide* will be presented in detail in the next chapters. These practices support the attributes of innovative systems and are rooted in the elements of change. Yet they are not "the magic bullet" or "the Holy Grail" for making schools relevant. They help create healthier, more vital systems, but they do not stand alone. They are part of a continuum of leadership behavior that supports improvement as well as innovation. The continuum represents the whole of leadership—there are times to be on one side, and there are times to be on the other. Because we need both improvement and innovation, the chapters in Part II are designed to honor this continuum of leadership behavior.

Paradoxes help the mind hold together opposing elements and create a deeper understanding of *the whole*—resisting the tendency to reduce things to their parts to understand their nature. In the chapters in Part II, we use paradoxes to help you develop a deeper understanding of each leadership practice and enhance your ability to move throughout the continuum as conditions in your organization dictate. In addition to giving you opportunities to develop a breadth of understanding, we also will be providing opportunities for you to develop your depth of understanding of these practices.

The four essential leadership practices stretch leadership capacity to the innovative side of the leadership continuum. Developing leadership capacities on this side requires a paradigm shift. It is a shift away from leadership expectations based solely in control to one where leaders use the life-giving properties of systems to promote adaptation. This side of the continuum is based in the principles of self-organization, where the attributes of innovation are at home. Moving into a new paradigm means moving into a new frontier of possibilities. Promise and potential are on the frontier; however, the exact forms they take are yet to be fully defined. For these reasons, this is not a how-to book—it can't be. The how-to is still emerging, still forming. This new frontier needs pioneers. As you read and use the activities to reflect on your leadership, look for opportunities to put some of the ideas to work in your practice. In this way, you actively participate in constructing your knowledge about what it will take for *you* and *your* organization to innovate, as well as improve.

Our hope is that some pioneering leaders are moved by the insights developed in Part II—moved to the point of action and that they are looking for other pioneers to connect with. To that end, we offer a vision of what is possible—one of potential and possibility. From this possibility, we hope that a community of practice forms—a community of practice where pioneering leaders can define together the how-to of this new paradigm. To encourage this, at the end of the book, we offer a means for you to connect and learn from one another by using a digital forum established as an online community in support of innovative school leadership.

Embrace
Dissonance

6

The things we fear most in organizations—fluctuations, disturbances, imbalances—need not be the signs of an impending disorder that will destroy us. Instead, fluctuations are the primary source of creativity.

—Margaret Wheatley, author and
management consultant

In nature, a system that thrives on chaos is dynamic and vital. On the other hand, a "stable" system is closest to entropy, which is closest to death.

—Phyllis Kirk, author and futurist

Instability is not just due to ignorance or incompetence but rather is a fundamental property of successful business systems. Successful managers use constrained instability in a positive way to provoke innovation.

—Ralph Stacey, author and
management expert

IN THIS CHAPTER

Part I, Leading Beyond Improvement, presented the case that as educational leaders work to keep their systems relevant, they are facing more and more challenges that require solutions from outside of current capacities. Bringing forth solutions outside of current capacity helps educational systems adapt to their changing environments. It is in those challenges that leadership is defined.

Helping systems chart new territory entices leaders to depart from present capacities to gain new insights and then to return to apply those insights to better the existing state of the system. This journey fits Campbell's (1991) characteristics of a heroic journey. On such a journey, the potential for transformation is proportional to the depth that one is able to uncover and bring alive his or her inner essence or the organization's core purpose, thus, the role of the courageous conversation.

> The more comfortable one is with dissonance, the more likely he or she is to use it as a creative force.

The hero's journey begins with departure, and dissonance creates the momentum for departure. Just as with great adventurers, the more comfortable one is with dissonance, the more likely he or she is to use it as a creative force. The secret to using it as a creative force is to be more and more attuned to the small disturbances. In this way, one is able to notice the disturbance when it is in an early stage rather than when it has grown to a full-scale, shake-you-to-the-core disturbance. Part of being adaptive is having the courage to move into disturbances rather than away from them and to do so early rather than late. This is why our first essential leadership practice is to *embrace dissonance*. This practice is derived from the change element of dissonance and the innovative attribute of choosing to be disturbed.

To start, a brief background for the important role dissonance plays in creating adaptation in the natural world is presented. The important role it plays in each of our lives follows. The contrast between these views of dissonance and the view of traditional organizations creates a continuum of leadership behavior that leaders must learn to navigate. Leadership how-to at the end of the continuum where the traditional organization resides is well documented by other sources.

Not as well documented is the end of the continuum representing the view of dissonance that is essential for adaptive, innovative organizations. Therefore, what leadership looks like at this end will be developed in more detail. Additionally, you will be provided with opportunities to reflect about how your leadership behavior moves on this continuum. Finally, some practical tips for increasing your ability to use dissonance as a creative force will be offered.

DISSONANCE IN THE NATURAL WORLD

In the previous chapter, we made the case that dissonance is vital to the change process, including it as one of four change elements. *By dissonance, we mean anything that causes fluctuation, perturbation, discomfort, or discord in the present state.* It can range from the look in a student's eyes, to a comment from a colleague, to an article about future work skills, to legislation regarding how the state funds public schools. Dissonance is anything that makes ripples in the status quo. It is anything that holds the potential to create disequilibrium in the system. When amplified, it is a force that can knock a system out of balance—not necessarily a bad thing.

Most of us cherish equilibrium in our personal lives and in our organizations. We do not want to be disturbed, and we perceive that something is wrong when systems are in states of disequilibrium. Yet disequilibrium is a natural part of life. Throughout the natural world, from the smallest entities to global systems things that are adapting and evolving go through cycles of equilibrium and disequilibrium. They need both because without periods of disequilibrium, systems stagnate and die.

Natural systems use cycles of equilibrium followed by periods of disequilibrium to stay on the adaptive edge. In this way, they generate varied and novel responses to conditions in their environment. These systems possess a deep underlying coherence, providing them structure and continuity, which holds them together. Yet within that coherence, there is dynamic fluctuation, allowing them to be ready to move into other states. This paradoxical state of stable yet malleable allows these systems to be "hungry" for disturbances to create richness and novelty. New information generates perturbations, ripples of energy that stimulate the system to create coherence and generate novel responses. Such systems are learning, adapting, and growing.

TAKE A MOMENT

What in your personal and professional life is creating ripples in the status quo?

Dissonance in Our Lives

We do not have to search far to find natural systems that work this way. The human brain is such a system. Our brains are constantly creating neural networks. They function in a way that wires and rewires those networks based on new information. To be healthy and to learn, the brain needs two things: routine and novelty. Routine is needed so that repetitious patterns can be easily recognized creating efficient neural networks. This is how we learn to speak and read, learn to recognize faces, and learn to find our way home. This is how most of our functioning and thinking occur. Routine also creates an element of safety, allowing for risk taking knowing that we can fall back on tried-and-true patterns. Routine alone, however, creates ruts where thinking can get stuck.

Novelty is unfamiliarity. To make sense of novel, unfamiliar information, the brain must develop new neural connections. So healthy, learning brains function in a state between stability and disorder where coherence is created through repetition and routine and where confusion and disorientation create novel, new neural connections, which are then reinforced with practice and routine.

This cycle is especially noticeable as we help children learn problem-solving skills. In our consulting work, we have demonstrated the need for routine and novelty to teachers by working with their students on a problem such as the one that involves a hen, a fox, and a bag of corn. A farmer must get them across a river using a boat but can only take one at a time. How does he do this without the fox eating the hen or the hen eating the corn? Take a moment yourself to think about it. (The answer is provided for you at the end of the chapter.)

What we find is that children attempt to solve this by applying sequential thinking: take the fox, leave it on the other side, go back and get the hen . . . and then get stuck. These patterns are so strong that they get caught in a rut and cannot visualize it any other way. When we introduce the *novel* concept that the farmer can take something back with him when he rows back, they solve the problem right away.

This pattern of stability followed by disequilibrium, in the right balance, is the foundation of the human experience. Think of how as kids we longed to throw ourselves into disequilibrium; from the swings on the playground to the roller coaster at the amusement park we sought it out. It was fun. It is what draws adolescents to risk and creates the rush of invincibility when they confront such a challenge. In growing to adulthood, we may have lost our taste for that childhood need to make ourselves dizzy and the adolescent desire for risk, yet we still value disequilibrium in other, more vicarious ways. Would you read a novel or watch a movie where the plot did not throw the hero or heroine into a state of disequilibrium? In fact, drama, adventure, and enlightenment are all responses to disequilibrium.

> In fact, drama, adventure, and enlightenment are all responses to disequilibrium.

In our personal lives, we know people, including ourselves, who say that their horrific illness was what moved them to a renewed sense of life, of spirit, and of motivation. This disequilibrium is essential for learning, and it moves us to higher states of awareness. It is also critical for healthy organizations.

Disequilibrium as an Ally

Organizationally, systems that function with disequilibrium as an ally are stabilized by a strong identity and core values, yet they are free enough to question, wonder, experiment, and hunger for learning within that identity. These are systems where people know why they are there and are free to act in that purpose to better the organization. These are systems where people possess high levels of autonomy yet are networked together with others, sharing a common vision and creating shared meaning. Such networked relationships help to create novelty and experimentation within the coherence of a common purpose. These systems innovate. Educators intuitively understand the importance of these concepts and approach them in schools when they create houses, learning teams, or communities of practice.

The systems (from biological to organizations) that use disequilibrium as a productive state are defined by several important characteristics. First, these systems know who they are, and they are highly sensitive to information that is discordant to that identity. Second, this form of *openness* fosters experimentation and possibilities in response to new information as part of creating meaning and answering the following fundamental questions: Is this important to my (our) survival, and what should I (we) do about it to better align with my (our) identity? The experimentation and learning generated by this dynamic allows the system to adapt to changes in its environment.

TAKE A MOMENT

When faced with disequilibrium does your organization view it as a productive state or not? Why or why not? What in the organization is contributing to this view of disequilibrium?

ESSENTIAL LEADERSHIP PRACTICE—EMBRACE DISSONANCE

The first of our leadership practices for creating innovation is to *embrace dissonance*. Why do we say *embrace* dissonance? Dissonance creates disequilibrium, and disequilibrium opens the door to innovation. Systems that adapt and thrive—that innovate—are those that seek novelty. Such systems welcome disturbance and use periods of disequilibrium as a creative force.

> Embracing dissonance means perceiving discordant information as an unexpected ally in the search for the nugget that refines into gold.

By encouraging you to embrace dissonance, we are not saying that you should respond to every discordant piece of information. To do so would make you reactive, create incoherence, and have you headed toward a nervous breakdown. *By embrace dissonance, we mean develop sensitivity to perturbations and notice information that is discordant with your current state.* By embrace dissonance, we mean to wonder—to be an explorer.

Explorers scan the horizon for the next great adventure—not for signs of impending doom. Embracing dissonance means perceiving discordant information as an unexpected ally in the search for the nugget that refines into gold. Those that embrace dissonance ask questions like, "What can this reveal?" "Where can this take us?" "How can this help us clarify where we stand with our mission?" Keep in mind that you are looking for the nugget. Embracing dissonance means to notice all of it in your *peripheral vision*—know it is there and then by referencing it against your purpose, beliefs, and vision filtering out the vast majority that does not cause some flutter, stirring, or perturbation when referenced. Filter until that special discord is found—the one that leads to reflection and transformation. You are seeking the bit of dissonance that keeps resonating as people determine what it means. It grows stronger, creating greater coherence the more people interact with it.

Think back to Randy's story in Chapter 3. As with every teacher and principal, there were all kinds of discordant information present at that time. There were district initiatives being implemented. There were difficult behaviors to deal with. There were state and national calls for change. There was a movement in the community for homeschooling among certain parents. There were other students with learning issues. There were contract concerns and changes in leadership at the top of the organization. All of the discord was in their peripheral vision. Yet with all of that discord, something in Randy's eyes resonated for the teacher and for her principal. That was the nugget to refine into gold.

Leaders who have learned to embrace dissonance have done so as a natural byproduct of a set of beliefs about change and how it occurs. They understand that change is about reordering and that transformative change is messy—it involves breaking down and letting go of old patterns so that new ones can emerge. They may not relish the messes, but they know that messes are an essential precursor to developing higher capacity. We have found that those leaders who are leading for innovation, do not just merely value dissonance and its role in change, they consciously choose to be disturbed, which is the first attribute of innovation. These leaders perceive that one of their main responsibilities is to disturb the status quo of the organization through creative tension. To them being comfortable with the status quo is a dangerous state. Creative tension comes from continually questioning, where are we headed? Where have we been? Where are we now? How are we going to get there?

TAKE A MOMENT

What is your personal view of change? How is your personal view of change contributing to improved learning for all students? Do you need to reexamine your perception of change?

Our first essential leadership practice for leading for innovation is to embrace dissonance. The relationship of these elements in their role in leading for innovation is shown in Figure 6.1.

Figure 6.1   Leading for Innovation—Embrace Dissonance

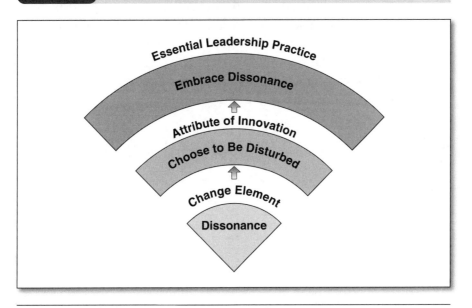

The Continuum of Leadership Behavior—Dissonance

Although it is essential to the process of innovation to embrace dissonance, we recognize that this is a truly difficult thing to do for most educational organizations. It is not that leaders of traditional organizations and those that work in them do not want change; they do—but they often strive for change without dissonance.

Superintendents, principals, and teachers learn quickly that those above them and around them do not like disequilibrium, so they work for change without making too many waves. Unfortunately, that important state between stability and disorder—the one where innovation occurs—cannot be achieved without dissonance. Avoiding dissonance means initiatives are sought that create minimal disruptions. These tend to be quick fixes and surface changes. Seeking such solutions eliminates the energy needed to break apart old ways so that new ways can form. Coherence is often lost as well. For educators, "the main problem is not the absence of innovations but the presence of too many disconnected, episodic, piecemeal, superficially adorned projects" (Fullan, 2001, p. 109).

At the heart of a leader's ability to embrace dissonance is a connection to an underlying belief that accepts the importance of the cycle of equilibrium followed by disequilibrium as a natural, healthy process. Yet the underlying mind-sets of traditional organizations do not recognize this cycle.

Command-and-control organizations value stability, and in this mind-set, initiatives are added on to or on top off what already exists. So a dilemma for educational leaders is to embrace dissonance in systems that value stability. To understand the spectrum of what leaders must deal with, we have created a continuum, which we call the Continuum of Leadership Behavior for Creating Change (see Resource C). Figure 6.2 reflects the dissonance concept on the continuum.

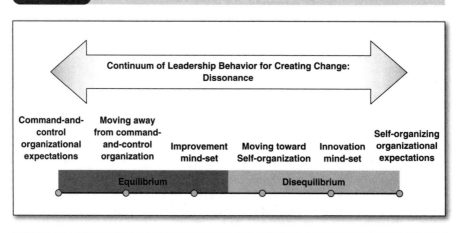

Figure 6.2   Continuum of Leadership Behavior—Dissonance

The reason this continuum contrasts command-and-control organizational expectations with self-organizing organizational expectations is that the attributes of innovation are compatible to self-organizing systems, and leaders work in organizations with policy and practices derived from command-and-control organizations. Most school organizations seem to recognize that the command-and-control structures of traditional organizations are not well suited to today's changing world. They have tried to incorporate management techniques that move away from pure forms of command-and-control in efforts to be responsive to change forces.

Some examples of this are site-based management, feedback and involvement from stakeholders, team approaches, data-driven decision making, goal setting, and learner-centered approaches. All of these are done because of a belief that involving others produces better results. Yet these endeavors are implemented without changing the mental model that is at the heart of command-and-control organizations: order needs to be imposed—it will not emerge naturally.

TAKE A MOMENT

What are your mind-sets about order and disequilibrium? What are your organization's mind-sets about order and disequilibrium? Do these mind-sets lead to your personal and organizational visions becoming a reality? Why or why not?

Unfortunately, for innovation in the command-and-control model, the stuff of "effective" leaders remains being good at control, predictability, policy, and procedures. In this mind-set, rather than embracing it, dissonance becomes something to avoid. Potential innovations are often squelched because things that look different create waves. Keeping the issues out of the newspapers and off the talk radio shows becomes the leader's focus. In actuality, allowing this may create the disturbance that is needed to move into dissonance and bring about substantive change.

Leaders face a dilemma when it comes to embracing dissonance: the need to recognize its vitally important role in creating innovation. Yet they are working in organizations that, at their roots, do not value it. No matter how much organizations attempt to push decision making down the organizational chain, it is nearly impossible for them to create innovation because the expectations for leaders are still rooted to a command-and-control mind-set. Innovation follows from dissonance that breaks down

Figure 6.3   Continuum of Leadership Behavior—Full Spectrum

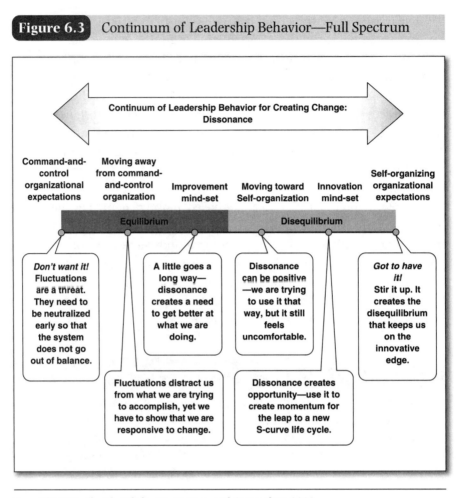

old ways, something completely adverse to the command-and-control mind-set. Therefore, we use the Continuum of Leadership Behavior for Creating Change (Figure 6.3) to reveal the full spectrum of leadership behavior involved in organizational change.

Attuned to the Importance
of Both Equilibrium and Disequilibrium

Depending on the circumstances, leaders will work at all points of the equilibrium/disequilibrium continuum. Earlier, we stated that leaders need to be "in it but not of it." By this, we mean that they need to survive in the command-and-control organization but not have their thinking be derived from that mind-set. Practically speaking, this means that they should rarely operate from the left end of the continuum and that the expectations of the traditional organization will make the right end seem too extreme. Therefore, most leadership behavior will move between the middle four points of the continuum.

Think of the S-curve life cycle. In the introduction phase of the life cycle, some level of dissonance helps emerging ideas strengthen and solidify. For example, a new method of reading instruction needs to be subjected to challenge and hard analysis to determine if it really produces better results than a previous method.

Once it is determined that the method is better, then the feedback needs to focus on implementation. Although some degree of dissonance is useful at this stage, it should be of a lesser degree so that the method has the best opportunity to take root. This is the time to commit to standardization—in other words to say, "This idea has proven itself. Now it is time to get on board."

At the mature stage of the life cycle, the method will be growing stagnant and not be adequately addressing emerging problems. At this stage, amplifying dissonance helps to create the energy needed to break apart the stagnating idea so that a new method can be developed. The relationship of the equilibrium/disequilibrium continuum to the S-curve is shown in Figure 6.4.

Being attuned to the importance of both equilibrium and disequilibrium is a must for leaders trying to create improvement and innovation. Much of leadership training has focused on the maintaining equilibrium

Figure 6.4 Dissonance and the S-Curve

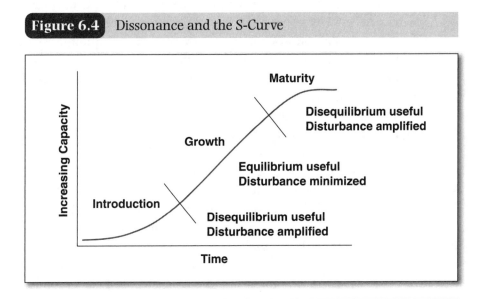

half of the continuum because the thinking that is at the root of command-and-control organizations values that aspect. That is not enough today. Leaders also have to develop better awareness and practice based on the disequilibrium side of the continuum.

WHAT EMBRACING DISSONANCE LOOKS LIKE IN PRACTICE

For now, we will assume that you are already well aware of what leaders do on the equilibrium side of the continuum. So at this time, we will help you develop a clearer picture of what leaders do on the disequilibrium side of the continuum. At the most fundamental level, embracing dissonance requires the willingness to yield to some degree of uncertainty. In our experience, we have found that those who lead for innovation possess a change orientation that perceives the state of uncertainty as a precursor to new understanding.

Opening up to uncertainty allows one to move into the unknown. It is saying, "I don't know, *yet*—but I trust that I will eventually figure it out." It incorporates a mind-set that disequilibrium is a temporary, necessary state. Yielding to uncertainty requires faith and confidence—trusting that after a period of not knowing, new insights, understandings, and solutions will emerge. Someone who embraces dissonance sees it as the possibility of wonder and adventure rather than angst and anxiety.

We also notice that those educators who embrace dissonance possess other characteristics. People who work with these types of educators describe them as being learners. They are not necessarily seen as a learner who has acquired more knowledge than anyone else, even though they may be very knowledgeable. They are described as learners who never stop making connections between their thinking and new ideas. As a result, they ask many questions. Their questioning is not random; however, it is always well timed and relevant. They seem to be able to ask a thought-provoking question at just the right time.

Leaders who embrace dissonance are also described as being genuine, confident, and trusting. They are self-assured yet humble because they know they cannot do it alone—they need others. Those they work with know what they stand for—and they know where they stand with him or her. The essence of these traits is captured in a quote from a superintendent we have worked with: "Trust is the key to continuity over time in establishing a quality learning environment for students. Leaders must depend on the expertise of others but the leader must hold everyone accountable for carrying out the shared expectations defined to provide quality learning." Educators who manifest these qualities use their energy and passion to create an environment where students thrive.

TAKE A MOMENT

What leaders have you met, worked with, or have known through other sources that possess the characteristics of embracing dissonance as described earlier? What have their organizations been able to do?

Using Dissonance as a Creative Force

To work toward integrating the behaviors on the Continuum of Leadership Behavior for Creating Change, it is time to ask, what will it take to help you become more comfortable with dissonance so that you can perceive it as a creative force? To start with, take some time to consider several courageous conversation starters. To do this, curl up in a reflective spot, take some time for a long walk in a private place, or get a pen and notebook to start a reflective journal—it is time to ponder the following:

- In the past month, where on the continuum has your leadership been? What is your tolerance for professional dissonance?
- When, if ever, do you consciously move to the disequilibrium side of the continuum? What does it feel like? How do others respond when you are there?
- Think back to recent dissonance you have experienced. Rerun it in slow motion. What happens in your mind and spirit when dissonance comes along? Do you find yourself moving into it or away from it? Why?

ACTION TIPS—EMBRACE DISSONANCE

Following are some tips to help you become more comfortable with the first leadership practice: *embrace dissonance.*

Your Discomfort Is Telling You Something About Your Beliefs

Whenever you feel some discomfort from discordant information, it is telling you something. Discordant information is discordant because it is perturbing one or more of your established beliefs. If it were not, it would not be discordant. So take time to notice the discord. Ask yourself, why does that bother me? Again, you could drive yourself crazy if you deeply analyze every piece of discordant information, but in asking the question, your mind and spirit open to it. Occasionally, a piece of discordant information will bounce around in your being. When it does, do not stay on the surface; ask yourself these questions:

- What belief is at the root of my discomfort?
- Is this belief still valid or do I need to modify it?

This can trigger a courageous conversation that starts you on a hero's journey. In this, you are opening up to what systems that are using the state between stability and instability are doing. Their identity is solid, yet they hunger for the perturbation that creates novel responses and deeper meaning.

Be Open to the Journey

By *the journey*, we mean developing capacities that move you and your organization to the adaptive edge. To be open to the journey, start by being open to mild disturbances and begin to think of them differently. Like most leaders, you probably have become very good at solving small problems for the people in your organization—so good that people probably reinforce your ability to do so. We are talking about the day-to-day things that people expect you to solve for them because taking care of them is what leaders are "supposed to do." In the classroom, this is children wanting the teacher to do their thinking. Administratively, this is a myriad of issues where people expect the leader to help maintain the status quo. Instead of taking charge and developing a quick fix, respond in an unexpected way. Respond in a way that might stimulate the formation of new neural connections. Respond with an answer like one of the following:

- I'm not sure I have an answer for that right now—let's both think about that.
- I'm thinking about why we are here, and I think we may want to think about what we are reinforcing if I respond in that way.
- What is the issue as you see it?

The point is to pause . . . to take the time to think and show others that it is important to look below the surface. By doing this, occasionally, you not only open the door to deeper connections for yourself, but you are also modeling an expectation for others to follow.

It's Not About You

Whenever dissonance comes along, it is a natural reaction to feel as if we are being judged by how we respond. It may be that we are judging ourselves or referencing how we think others expect us to respond. By doing this, we personalize the dissonance. When we personalize the disso- nance, we become defensive, and in doing so, ego can begin to play a part in our response. Most dissonance is not about you. Our experience has taught us that, even though it may be hard to grasp at first, we are a part of something larger. It is important to recognize a broad perspective as you face dissonance. Many expect you, as the leader, to make it go away instead of embracing it. When this happens, the focus can shift from the issue at hand to the response.

Keep your focus on the big picture and help others reframe their think- ing around the larger context of the dissonance. To help others see beyond themselves, ask yourself, what aspect of a larger whole is activating a sense of responsibility within me? Then nurture others to activate a similar sense of responsibility.

> What aspect of a larger whole is activating a sense of responsibility within me?

So when you find yourself ready to react negatively to disso- nance, remind yourself, "It's not about me." This little statement can help you move your awareness from an egocentric position to one of being part of something larger. Even a little shift in that direction is helpful to unlock- ing the door to openness. In this way, dissonance can become an ally for moving to a higher capacity rather than to be a personal threat.

PARADOXICAL LEADERS

Perhaps the best way to describe those recognized as leading for improve- ment and innovation is to refer to them as paradoxical leaders. In a narrow view, their behavior may appear to be contradictory, but these people work the whole spectrum. When one considers the whole of anything, it can appear to be contradictory because the whole contains both ends of the spectrum. After all, when it comes to dissonance, we are saying that leaders need to be able to protect against dissonance yet embrace it. To lead from the full spectrum is to appear to be paradoxical. To those who have integrated it, it is not paradoxical—it is being complete. One way to help you become more limber in moving across the continuum is to not only help you understand the two sides of the continuum better but also to help you become a para- doxical leader in regard to dissonance. To help you not want dissonance at the same time you are able to embrace it, we invite you to integrate the fol- lowing paradoxical statement into your job description. As a paradoxical leader who leads for both improvement and innovation, one component of your job description is to *hold the system together while you help it break apart.*

Hold the System Together While You Help It Break Apart

What this means is to be aware of the organization's core values, purpose, and other elements that should remain constant over time. Once these are clarified, honor them, for they hold your system together. Yet also be ready to help the ways in which those things are manifested change with the times. To do this, leaders need to help old manifestations break apart so new manifestations and meanings can form. For example, it will probably always be important for schools to develop students who are literate. However, what it means to be literate is not the same today as is was 10 years ago—nor will today's meaning be what is needed 10 years from now.

With this leadership paradox in mind, it helps you keep an adaptive perspective on things. It helps you know that dissonance works to update how you and your organization manifest what is truly important. At the same time, when what is important is perturbed, it helps you clarify and recommit to the essence of why you hold these things to be important. So it is essential for leaders to develop the ability to break apart old views and established practices that prevent the system's core values and purpose from adapting in a healthy relationship with the external environment.

Leading in this way is not as paradoxical as it may first seem. Think of being raised by your parents or raising your own children. There were (are) times when discipline and a firm stance were (are) needed—and times when compassion and tenderness were (are) in order. These are not incompatible, separate entities; they are aspects of the whole of parenting.

What is important is that the journey to achieve leadership that embraces stability and instability starts with you. It starts with thinking about the people you influence in your system—whether they are in a classroom, school, district, or university. Your journey begins with an idea of why this is important and taking a first step. To help start your journey to achieving a healthy balance to holding the system together and helping it break apart, take some time to reflect on the following questions:

- What are the core values and beliefs that define your leadership? Have those beliefs evolved over the years? If so, what caused them to evolve?
- What are the core values and beliefs that define what is important to your system? (Think of your system as being your classroom, school, district, or university.) Have those beliefs evolved over the years? If so, what caused them to evolve?
- In your system, how are people encouraged to let go of old, unproductive beliefs and practices? What could you do to make this a healthier expectation in your system?

- In your personal life, how do you balance *holding together what is important* and *breaking it apart* so that it can evolve? Are there any suggestions your personal, adaptive self can make to your professional, adaptive self? Vice versa?

SUMMARY

The first of the essential leadership practices for leading for improvement and innovation is embrace dissonance. This is an essential practice because dissonance is needed to break down old patterns and create movement from one S-curve life cycle to a new one. This movement is the essence of innovation.

Dissonance creates healthy systems through introducing periods of disequilibrium to states of equilibrium. Instead of something to be feared, disequilibrium is a natural, temporary occurrence for systems. Without it, systems stagnate and die.

As healthy as it is, it is still something undervalued in most traditional organizations. Today's educational leaders face a dilemma: Embracing dissonance is essential for helping organizations innovate, yet it is not valued in many systems. As leaders are faced with *being in it but not of it*, it is helpful for them to consider their movement across the Continuum of Leadership Behavior for Creating Change. In this way, they can become more aware of when to reinforce stability in the system and when to embrace dissonance to move toward innovation. In the next chapter, we will develop our second essential leadership practice: *create context.*

SBK High School: Embracing Dissonance

The leaders of SBK High School have shown that they are willing to embrace dissonance as a key practice. Currently, the high school is being disturbed as it learns more about the urgency facing education and learning more about the needs of and for the students. The high school principal is facilitating conversations among the staff as a by-product of the Schools for the Future initiative. She notices that her approach is different now—she says things to her staff such as, "We are on a journey with an unknown end, but it is essential and critical that this journey be taken." In collaborative work sessions, staff can be overheard discussing the changing needs of learners. Teachers are more open in talking with students about how they learn. Reference is made to the future needs of learners as decisions are being made. A sense of urgency is being felt.

The high school has been working on aligning standards and developing common end-point assessments and piloting alternative grading practices. Although they have been doing this for several years, it is only now that teachers are experiencing a disturbance, seeing the value of the work and wanting more quality time to get the work done. When the staff began to question how to best use professional time, the superintendent empowered a team to investigate the need and develop solutions to present to their colleagues. In the past, a quick fix would have been expected.

Additionally, a technology-driven reading support program that provides evidence of student results is changing the focus of what teachers are expected to do. This was originally an improvement initiative. Yet as people are beginning to use dissonance as a creative force, the way it is being implemented is beginning to move it beyond improvement. A cross-curricular collaborative team of ninth-grade teachers is using the reading program more broadly to improve reading comprehension. An intense intervention approach is being used with students who are identified in need. However, this is not at the expense of a rich, broad curriculum experience but as part of it. Little disturbances through conversations are challenging the ways business is being done in this high school. The leaders are embracing dissonance—and are helping the staff to do so as they go about their work.

TEAM CONVERSATION STARTERS

As a team, take the time to share your responses to the reflective questions in the "Increasing Your Ability to Use Dissonance as a Creative Force" and the "Paradoxical Leaders" sections of this chapter. What common patterns emerge from this dialogue? What more would you like to do with or learn about these patterns?

Answer for the "hen, fox, and bag of corn" problem:

The farmer takes the hen across. Then he returns to get the fox. He takes the fox across. He leaves the fox and returns with the hen, rowing to the side of origin. There he leaves the hen and takes the bag of corn. He goes to the other side where he leaves the corn with the fox. He then returns for the hen. He picks up the hen and returns to the other side where the fox and bag of corn await him. How did you do?

Self-Assessment
Embrace Dissonance

For this self-assessment, we ask you to consider the level to which you value, as you face and deal with dissonance, the spectrum of elements listed below. Go through them once making a mark for where you balance them in your personal life. Go through a second time making a different mark for where you balance them in your professional life. What differences, if any, do you notice and why?

Equilibrium	◆——◆——◆——◆——◆——◆	Disequilibrium
Predictability	◆——◆——◆——◆——◆——◆	Novelty
Coherence	◆——◆——◆——◆——◆——◆	Ambiguity
Holding things together	◆——◆——◆——◆——◆——◆	Letting them break apart
Need for control	◆——◆——◆——◆——◆——◆	Yield to uncertainty
Knowing	◆——◆——◆——◆——◆——◆	Discovering
Security	◆——◆——◆——◆——◆——◆	Adventure
Improvement	◆——◆——◆——◆——◆——◆	Innovation

Create Context   **7**

The many policies and procedures that are being advanced today in the name of school improvement are so numerous and varied that, for many, they are simply a blur of confusion.

—Lawrence Lezotte, author and educator

If we want people to be innovative, we must discover what is important to them, and we must engage them in meaningful issues.

—Margaret Wheatley, author and management consultant

Leaders need to build and maintain a shared purpose while encouraging enough creative diversity to ensure continued growth for students and staff.

—Terrence Deal and Kent Peterson, authors and educators

IN THIS CHAPTER

This chapter will develop the background for understanding the second essential leadership practice necessary for evolving organizations that balance improvement and innovation: *create context.* This practice is derived from the change element of identity and the innovative attribute of self-referencing. To start the presentation of this leadership practice, a brief background for the important role identity plays in creating adaptation in the natural world will be developed. The important role it plays in each of our lives will also be discussed. The continuum of leadership behavior as it relates to organizational identity will be presented. Additionally, you will be provided with opportunities to reflect on how your leadership behavior moves on this continuum. Finally, some practical tips for increasing your ability to create the context needed for balancing improvement and innovation will be offered.

THE IMPORTANCE OF IDENTITY

In Chapter 5, we made the case that identity is vital to the change process, and we included it as one of the change elements. In the natural world, from molecules to ecosystems, individual, independent entities form systems by organizing around a shared intent or common purpose. At the heart of this forming is an axiom that together more is possible. It is this shared intent that forms a system's identity. *By identity, we mean the shared intent that creates a system's "sense of self."* It is a factor in any change process because "in deciding what to do, a system will refer back to its sense of self" (Wheatley, 2005, p. 37).

The Importance of Identity in the Natural World

Every natural system has to account for changes in its external environment. If it does so in a way that allows it to remain in a healthy relationship with its environment, it survives. If it does not, it begins to lose its relevance and starts to drop off the evolutionary radar screen. In nature, the way a system accounts for changes in its environment is through taking in new information and referencing that against the

> Each system needs to determine if this new information is important to its survival and, if so, how to respond.

system's *sense of self*—its identity. Each system needs to determine if this new information is important to its survival and, if so, how to respond. A response is required when the system is perturbed in relation to how it understands its needs.

Does the external stimulus threaten the system's understanding of itself and its needs? Or does it enhance the system's understanding of this? The clearer the system's sense of self, the more efficiently the process of referencing new information against that identity aids its ability to remain vital. As a metaphor for this concept, think of a school of fish. Each member of the school is a unique individual. Yet together they gain stability and protective advantages by moving as one. As the school moves, its form is dynamic, changing, and modifying based on changes in the surrounding conditions, yet as a whole, it remains a school.

As mentioned previously, systems that are evolving are termed on the edge of chaos where they possess an identity that paradoxically blends stability and instability. In these systems, a deep underlying coherence provides structure and continuity for the individual entities of the system. Each entity uniquely interprets new information entering the system, yet the meaning of that information is developed in relationship to the shared identity. This means that such a system uses its identity to stabilize and hold itself together while allowing for changes and adaptations within the system.

Animals and humans are living examples of this concept. Although the body of an animal or human maintains its form as a whole, at the cellular level, it is changing dramatically as new cells throughout the body are being replaced daily. In a matter of months, both animals and humans have bodies that consist of entirely new cells. Illustrated here is the idea that, as a whole, the system is stable, held together by its identity, yet it is subjected to many changes and adaptations at the "local" level.

Stable on the whole-system level and dynamic and fluctuating on the local, individual entity level—it is this combination of systemic identity along with the fluctuation and change exhibited by the individual entities that gives the system its sustainability. So throughout the natural world, the concept of identity, or a system's sense of self, is used to create stability and to contain fluctuation and variation to create systemic vitality. The concept of identity and its relation to systemic vitality is also found in our personal lives.

The Importance of Identity in Our Lives

The concept of stability at the whole-system level while allowing fluctuation at the local level should be very familiar to us. In our lives, this relationship is the starting place for learning. Learning is about making meaning—referencing new information against existing understanding creates meaning. On the whole-system level, this understanding is stable. Yet to learn, we need to have fluctuations on the local level—the level of our neurons. As our brains take in new information, we are determining the importance of that information to our being based on answering the following questions: Does this new information make sense? And does it have meaning for my identity? If the answers are affirmative, then the new information has a chance to perturb the established sense of self and be connected to existing patterns. If it does perturb our neural connections, then we must notice it and make sense of it. We must form new meaning by connecting it to existing meaning. This is how we learn. And at the heart of learning is our identity—our sense of self—for this is the filter that is referenced when we decide whether information is important.

Our identity reveals itself through our egos, our experiences, our mental models, and our past learning. A healthy identity is one that creates stability overall but allows for fluctuation and wonder. This relationship of new information referenced against our identity works in all of our lives. Think back to John in Chapter 5

> A healthy identity is one that creates stability overall but allows for fluctuation and wonder.

and how his life changed when he used existing meaning to create new meaning for his professional life and his personal identity. A quote attributed to Alfred North Whitehead (Whitehead quoted in Harigopal, 2001) about progress is just as meaningful, if we substitute the words "adaptation" for progress and "identity" for order: "The art of progress (adaptation) is to preserve order (identity) amid change and to preserve change amid order (identity)" (Harigopal, p. 2, parenthetical statements added).

Adaptation in living systems depends on having a strong, yet malleable identity—and the same is true for organizations. In organizations that balance improvement and innovation, identity is established through a clear purpose, a commonly shared vision, mutual principles, and a culture where people are *pleased but never satisfied*. Districts and schools that balance improvement and innovation have developed a dynamic identity that is strong enough to hold everyone together around a common purpose (one referenced before the interests of a department or trusted colleagues). This purpose is the self-referencing attribute of innovation that allows people to question, wonder, experiment, and hunger for learning within that identity.

As we said earlier, and want to emphasize again, these are systems where people know why they are there and are free to act within that purpose to better the organization. These are systems where people possess levels of autonomy yet are networked together with others, sharing a common vision and creating shared meaning. Such networked relationships help create novelty and experimentation within the coherence of a common purpose. These systems innovate.

The role identity plays in helping organizations evolve, perhaps, can be best understood by examining what is happening in systems that are not adapting. In these organizations, two aspects of their identity prevent adaptive growth: (1) Their organizational identity is too rigid, or (2) their organizational identity is too loose.

When the organization's identity is too rigid, the collective identity overpowers the autonomy of individuals. Referencing new information against a rigid identity produces very little systemic perturbation—the dissonance systems need for sparking adaptive response. In other words, there is little freedom or room to develop novel behavior because the individual entities are confined too tightly by a rigid, rule-bound identity. These organizations feel repressive to those who work in them. Bureaucratic structures, rigid policy, and past practice are the reference points when new information and ideas try to penetrate the operations. These organizations hold tight to a fixed identity creating a false sense that they are protected from changes in the external world.

The other condition is where the organization's identity is too loose, not clearly defined, or not strong enough to hold the individuals together.

This means that there is not a strong enough identity for the individuals to reference new information against to answer the following question: Is this new idea important to the system's vitality? Instead, the answer to that question is derived from the perspective of the individual: Is this new idea important to me? An individual may be perturbed by the information, but the system is not. In these cases, the system eventually ceases to be a system because the common thread that holds the individuals together is too weak.

Organizations that respond to every new idea as if it were important fit this description. Also fitting it are ones where people relate only to a *department or grade-level identity* rather than a systemwide identity. In each case, the organization's identity is not strong enough to hold the individuals together so that the adaptive advantages of the whole system can be realized. Below is an illustration that shows how a system's identity relates to its ability to adapt and evolve.

TAKE A MOMENT

Where do you think your system's identity lies in Figure 7.1? What evidence do you have to support your view?

Figure 7.1 System Identity

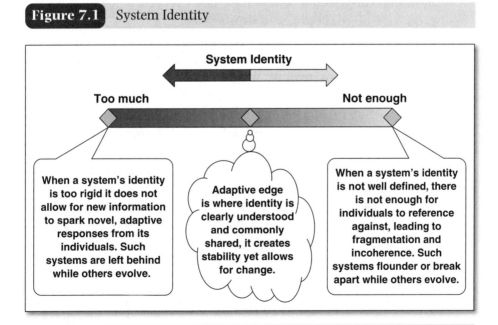

ESSENTIAL LEADERSHIP PRACTICE—CREATE CONTEXT

The second leadership practice for creating systems that balance improvement and innovation is to *create context*. This practice has to do with a leader's conscious, continuous effort to make the identity a dynamic reference point for everyone in the organization. *What we mean by create context is leaders consciously working to create a context where a clear, coherent identity can be grown and cultivated every day.* In this sense, think of the leader as a gardener and that the identity is the garden that needs tending and nurturing every day. Creating context is a leader's efforts to make visible the collective intentions and desires of the people associated with the organization—in a living way, not just as a statement on the wall. The aim is to make the identity a dynamic reference that frees individuals to work, create meaning, and share learning within that common purpose.

In a powerful, unsettling example, Wheatley (2006) brings to our attention that these elements form the basis of one of the most successful and adaptive world organizations—terror networks.

> Although these groups appear leaderless, they in fact are well-led by their passion, rage, and conviction. They share an ideal or purpose that gives them a group identity and which compels them to act. . . . They act free of constraints, encouraged to do "what they think is best" to further the cause. This combination of shared meaning with freedom to determine one's actions is how systems grow to be more effective and well-ordered. (¶ 41)

The idea of terror networks, in and of itself, is frightening and unsettling. Even more disturbing is thinking of their organizational techniques for empowering adaptive behavior as a good illustration of today's effective organizations. Yet unfortunately, there is no better example of what is achievable when a powerful, commonly shared purpose combines with the freedom to create meaning within that purpose. The point is raised to demonstrate the power that is possible when identity is a clearly articulated reference for determining what is important.

Let us present a more positive example; think back to Randy's story in Chapter 3. The conference between Randy's mother, the teacher, and the principal started out like hundreds of thousands of such conferences held in schools annually. Concerns about Randy's performance were presented to the mother. In response, she was properly concerned about his learning and was waiting for the professionals to prescribe the cure. What made this conference different for Randy was that at the point when the teacher and principal usually say, "Here is what we are going to do about it," or "Here is what you need to do about it," they said, "We are not sure what to do about it, but we will figure it out." It was at precisely this point that this meeting became more than the usual conference. The teacher and principal could not give a pat answer because when Randy's situation was referenced against the school's identity—they couldn't.

Randy's situation could not be resolved with current practice, so the organization's sense of self was perturbed. The only way to deal with this perturbation was to develop a response that resolved the conflict between organizational identity and student performance. This is the effect a strong identity has when it is the reference for determining what is important. The leadership practice create context follows from the change element of identity and self-referencing—an attribute of innovation. This relationship is shown in Figure 7.2.

Figure 7.2   Leading for Innovation—Creating Context

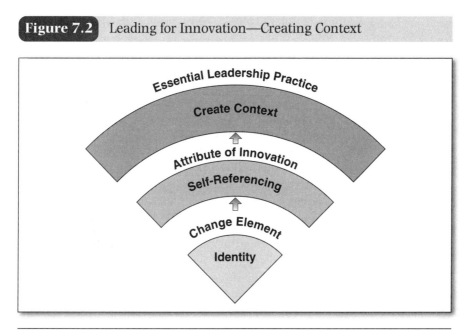

The Continuum of Leadership Behavior Regarding Identity

School leaders inherently realize the importance of a shared identity, which is why so many resources are spent to develop vision and mission statements. It is also why goals are set and committees are created—so that everyone can get on the same page. Creating a strong identity takes time, diligence, and continuous effort. It takes a deep commitment to processes that create order and meaning through dialogue around important issues. Hardest of all for traditional leaders, it requires letting go of control so that the meaning of a shared purpose is genuine and authentic—so that it truly belongs to everyone and inspires commitment to that purpose.

We recognize that creating the context to foster improvement and innovation is easier said than done for most educational organizations. This work is hard to do because, to get there, we have to go deeper than we are used to going. Leaders are acclimatized to directing and managing people, not connecting them and trusting that they share common aspirations. Often, the deeper work of creating common purpose seems soft and a waste of time when leaders are under pressure to get things done. Frankly, because of the nature of command and control, leaders of traditional organizations find it easier to create policy and procedures than to create the shared intent that fosters an inspiring sense of purpose.

The world today is complex and demands that to understand issues we must go beyond *either-or* thinking. Yet what we have found is that the more complex things become, the more people want things to be simplified and stabilized. And policies and procedures are the quick fixes for stabilizing situations. Ironically, as things become more complex, it is a simple, clear identity that creates coherence, not quick fixes.

A dilemma for leaders wanting to create an identity that fosters the conditions for both improvement and innovation is that they need to respect the important role policy and procedures play for people at the same time they realize that a clear, coherent identity will more likely release the potential of people so that the school can adapt to the complex demands of society. With this in mind, we offer the leadership continuum for identity presented in Figure 7.3.

When one first examines the two main groupings of this spectrum, it looks as if *policy and product* are mutually exclusive to a *sense-making process*. They are not. It is more accurate to think of them being present at the same time with one overlaying the other. The challenge for leaders is to understand the full spectrum and know when to bring each characteristic to the forefront.

To illustrate, think of the S-curve life cycle again. As we have mentioned before, in this life cycle, there are times when new ideas have emerged and are beginning to grow. This is the growth stage of the life cycle. It is a time to standardize promising ideas. At these times, policy and an emphasis on product can be useful. Policy creates consistency, which is good for standardizing a product. It works well for straightforward tasks in stable environments. It is through the growth stage that the tasks are relatively straightforward and the system is somewhat stable—as it relates to the improvement of the new ideas. These are times when feedback and data are important to making adjustments. At this stage, the perturbations are

Figure 7.3 Continuum of Leadership Behavior—Identity

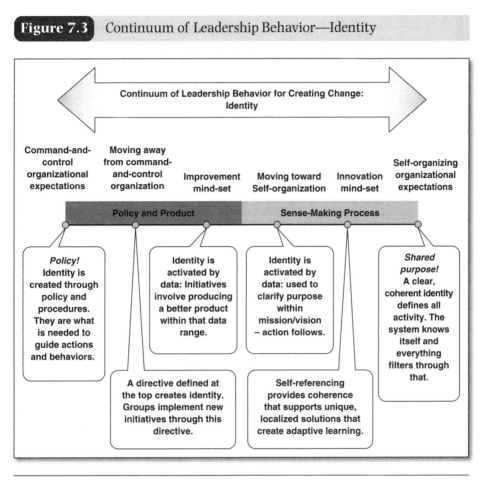

relative to the new ideas more than the identity, so the reference is of a rein-forcing nature, not a challenging one. During this time, working to unify practice through policy or procedure can be productive. Bringing these to the forefront of practice does not mean that the leader loses sight of the shared purpose.

However, it is also important to recognize that the very thing that makes policy work can also work against it. Policy-driven identities are not good for times when adaptation is needed. Think of the introduction and maturity phases of the S-curve growth cycle. At these times, pertur-bations are important. At the introduction stage, perturbations refer-enced against a clear identity are important for shaking out which emerging ideas are the strongest. Also, at the maturation stage, pertur-bations are necessary to create the energy for breaking apart old ideas so new ones can form.

When perturbations are important, referencing a clear identity is more essential than referencing policy and past practice. A shared purpose holds the system together and allows for novel responses when the system is perturbed. Policy and procedure cannot do this. At these times, it is important for leaders to draw on the mind-sets on the right half of the continuum while respecting past practice. These relationships are shown in Figure 7.4.

Figure 7.4   Self-Referencing and the S-Curve

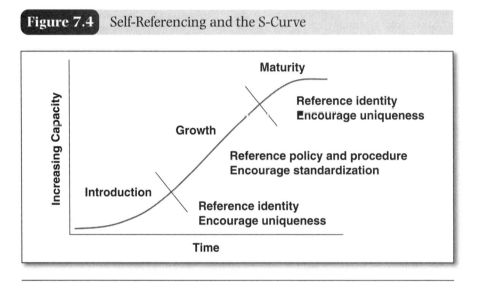

Being attuned to the importance of both the *product* and *process* sides of the continuum is necessary for leaders trying to create the context for improvement and innovation. Much of leadership training has focused on the maintaining policy and product half of the continuum because the thinking that is at the root of command-and-control organizations values that aspect. That is not enough today. Leaders also have to develop better awareness and practice based on the sense-making process side of the continuum to create the best conditions for an identity that values improvement and innovation.

WHAT CREATING CONTEXT LOOKS LIKE IN PRACTICE

Expert gardeners know the unique characteristics of their garden and artfully create the conditions that get the most out of the garden. In a similar manner, creating the context for improving and innovating is best achieved in a paradoxical blend of structure and freedom. To create the right conditions, leaders are always considering when it is best to afford the system the structure it needs through referencing policy and procedures and when it is best to create freedom through referencing a shared vision and shared purpose and giving individuals the space to do what they think is best within that.

So what is it that draws people in and makes them want to connect to an organizational identity? In nature, systems form around a shared intent. More is possible when linked than when done individually. The same is true for people. They want to be connected to organizations where they can share a common intent. We have found that while people like to be individuals, they also have a deep need to belong—so that their individuality can connect to something larger. When we realize that others are seeking common intent, it becomes clear that an organizational identity dominantly formed by interacting with our policies and practices is likely to be an uninspiring one to people.

> As counterintuitive as it might seem . . . the best way to lead people into the future is to connect with them deeply in the present. The only visions that take hold are shared visions—and you will create them only when you listen very, very closely to others, appreciate their hopes, and attend to their needs. (Kouzes & Posner, 2009)

Most noticeable in the leaders we have worked with who create the context for a well-articulated, commonly shared identity is that they are connectors. They encourage connections in others, but it starts with them. Perhaps because of the nature of such leadership, we notice that these leaders use reflection to diligently align their beliefs and actions. They constantly seek to connect policy with purpose and to balance product and process. They do this through continuous reflection and using feedback to monitor their actions. We notice that they do not necessarily withdraw to a quiet place to be by themselves to reflect. They are reflecting on the go—switching their mental awareness from the microview to the macroview. Through this process, they challenge themselves and those they interact with to act from expanding understandings of their sense of self, expanding understandings of their individual and organizational identity.

Others also describe leaders who create meaningful context as being trusting and trustworthy. They clarify intent and trust others to do what is best within that. They encourage risk-taking and are tolerant of mistakes and miscues as long as the mistakes have been made within the context of the organization's identity. People like being around and working with these leaders because they stand for something. These leaders know who they are and why they are there. Most important, they help others work from a sense of deeper commitment. Perhaps, what people respect most about them is that the leaders honor them as individuals and allow them to link their individuality with their need to belong to and contribute to something meaningful.

These leaders stand out because their behavior helps people clarify and come in contact with the organization's identity—why it exists. Even more important, their behavior helps people actively shape this identity into a common intent that becomes the reference for their actions. People in systems led by these leaders are connected to a larger good and feel empowered knowing they can act within that to better the organization.

Increasing Your Ability to Create Context

To work toward integrating the behaviors on the Continuum of Leadership Behavior for Creating Change (Resource C), it is time to ask, what will it take to help you become more comfortable with creating the context for balancing product and process? Once again, let us start by taking some time to consider several courageous conversation starters. To do this, go back to that reflective spot, take some time for that long walk in a private place, or revisit your reflective journal—it is time to consider the following:

- What is your organization's sense of self? How do new people assimilate that organizational identity? What policies help that? What policies get in the way of that? What processes help that? What processes get in the way of that?
- When, if ever, do you consciously move to the process over product side of the continuum? What does it feel like? How do others respond when you are there?
- What is important to the people you lead? How do you help others create the context for their work? How do you help them explore and clarify their intentions and desires before going to work on a project, task, or initiative?

ACTION TIPS—CREATE CONTEXT

Following are some tips for helping you become more comfortable with our second essential leadership practice: create context.

Think of the Pebble in the Pond

Recall the image of a still pond with a surface as smooth as glass. Then think of this image as a pebble is dropped into it. The result is a circular ripple emanating out in a broadening 360° wave. Now, associate this image with a leader's role in creating context. In essence, creating context is helping people's perceptions broaden like the wave created by the pebble in the pond. Leaders are trying to help people connect their work to broader concepts and a richer sense of responsibility. Creating context means helping people expand beyond narrow, egocentric interpretations to broader understandings and commitments. By doing this, people are more likely to connect with deeper reasons for the work they are doing, and they are more likely to develop passion and a shared sense of purpose.

For example, in helping people understand the need for developing better assessments for student learning, leaders could choose to talk about how new assessments are needed to help measure student performance. Or they could choose to focus on how student performance is enhanced by developing a deeper understanding and an enriched use of assessments. In the first perspective, what are being changed are the assessments. This perspective is likely to produce convergent thinking as people accept the challenge and begin to focus on identifying the parts that need to be in place for it to happen. What is being changed in the second perspective is people's understanding of assessment and its role in enhancing student performance.

People are more likely to seek solutions to this challenge through divergent thinking as they expand their understanding of their role in creating effective assessment. Would you rather work on developing an assessment with others or work with them to enhance student learning through developing a richer understanding and practice of assessment? The pebble in the pond is a reminder to leaders to shape issues in a manner that broadens people's perspectives and helps them tap into deeper commitments.

Be the Identity

It starts with you, the leader. There is nothing more important than to live the meaning of the organization's identity. Most important, live it in a manner that says, "I'm not there, yet; I'm still interpreting its meaning." This gives you a sense of wonder, which is the catalyst for stretching beyond your current capacity—and even more important, it helps others stretch as well. Influential leadership guru Tom Peters (2005) believes that "Great Leaders are not (merely) great at 'leading.' They are great at inducing others to take novel journeys to . . . Places of Surpassing Importance" (p. 60).

People interpret meaning through your actions. When they see you "walking the talk" and inviting others to take the walk with you, powerful things happen. For example, part of your school's stated identity may be that "students come first." When people see you living that by challenging the system to operationalize these words into action, on both the small and large scale, they align to that as well because a tangible image of what it means is being shaped.

Be the identity also means that it becomes who you are. The large scale, overarching values of the identity becomes who you are. We say this because these overarching values are most assuredly ones longed for in every organization by the people in them. May we suggest that as a leader, you begin the journey to becoming the identity by combining two overarching values into one whole, such as to stand for structure and freedom or to commit to autonomy and belonging. In this way, becoming the identity becomes your journey. Think back to Chapter 1 where we presented Michelle's vision to create a school that makes a difference. To this day, she continues to focus all that she does on the identity of the school as one meeting the students' needs in a very diverse, multicultural learning community.

> Becoming the identity becomes your journey.

Cultivate the Culture

Cultivate the culture means that your responsibility is to create the conditions where people can feel committed to their work as well as to the success of the whole system. Relationships are at the heart of being able to do this. Relationships are essential to both individual effectiveness and group effectiveness. Sometimes, we think it's the big things that make a difference, but it's the culmination of all the little things that nurturing leaders do every day that helps to build productive relationships within an organization.

Cultivating the culture means that you commit to creating connections between individuals and groups in every way possible. Remember that a spark of innovation can be created when information connects in new ways. Just what is created and when it will spark is unpredictable. So increase the odds of that happening by encouraging people to connect across the organization in every way possible. Something as simple as having committees and teams made up of staff from different schools and grade/department levels across the prekindergarten through Grade 12 spectrum can bring forth a burst of new information and creative ways to energize issues and novel solutions. Always be conscious of helping the system connect with itself. This is how learning grows and how the possibility for the emergence of novel approaches is increased. Creating meaning around diverse perspectives also broadens the view of people—increasing the possibility that shared meaning will be developed.

Cultivating the culture also places you in the mind-set of being the gardener and helps others garden with you. Together you are growing the hopes, aspirations, and shared intentions of the organization. Your work is to create the conditions where people grow together doing important work that allows them to harvest both common and personal meaning—bettering them and making them feel good about themselves and others as well as the system. "I believe it's clear . . . CRYSTAL CLEAR . . . that people are attracted to . . . and retained by . . . institutions that . . . MAKE THEM FEEL GOOD ABOUT THEMSELVES AS HUMAN BEINGS" (Peters, 2005, p. 137).

PARADOXICAL LEADERS

The very aspect of the role identity plays in nature can be said to be paradoxical—to create stability on the whole-system level and allow for fluctuation on the local level. Possessing the identity that allows an organization to adapt and evolve means that leaders need to create the context for that identity in a manner that creates stable, productive work environments at the same time it allows for fluctuation and the development of novel responses to situations. Keep in mind, this is an age when schools are attempting to create a learning product that meets a standard of quality; at the same time, the world is demanding greater customized answers to individual needs. How can a school or district *standardize while individualizing* if its identity does not create stability *and* the room for the development of novel responses?

Once again, to those who have integrated the need for stability and fluctuation into how they create context, these are not separate aspects but rather part of the same whole of leadership. To help you move these concepts into a unified whole, it is important for you to start by becoming limber in moving across the continuum. To create the context for developing an identity that offers stability on the large scale and the space for fluctuation at the local level, we invite you to integrate the following paradoxical statement into your job description: Preserve your organizational identity, yet be ready to help it evolve into something more.

Preserve Your Organizational Identity, yet Be Ready to Help It Evolve Into Something More

To help start your journey to achieving a healthy balance preserving your organizational identity and readying yourself to help it evolve into something more, reflect on the following:

- How would you define your professional identity? Has that identity evolved over the years? How do you create the context for your personal identity to evolve?

- How would you define your system's identity? (Think of your system as being your classroom, school, district, or university.) What artifacts do others encounter that shape their perception of your system's identity? How does it evolve?
- As a leader, how do you create stability on the whole-system level and encourage the freedom to respond to perturbations on the local level?

SUMMARY

The second of our essential leadership practices for leading for improvement and innovation is create context. Creating context is about helping people articulate and connect to the organization's identity and giving them the opportunity to create meaning within that identity. This is an essential practice because identity is an important element of adaptive systems. In such systems, identity creates stability on the whole-system level, yet it acts as a reference for the perturbations and fluctuations that create novel responses on the local level. This is an important concept for organizations that are seeking to innovate and stay on the adaptive edge.

Schools that possess these characteristics create context by referencing a coherent, well-articulated, and deeply understood shared purpose. An identity based on a common shared purpose is one where people know why they are there and are free to act within that purpose to better the organization. These are systems where people possess levels of autonomy yet are networked together with others, sharing a common vision and creating shared meaning. Such networked relationships help to create novel responses to problems within the coherence of the school's common purpose.

Creating a context that allows organizations to both improve and innovate can be thought of as being paradoxical because it involves creating structure so that consistency can be developed while allowing perturbations and fluctuations to create novel responses. To create the conditions for both aspects to flourish, it is helpful for leaders to consider their movement across the Continuum of Leadership Behavior for Creating Change as it relates to identity. In this way, they can become more aware of when to reinforce structure and consistency in the system and when to encourage fluctuation to move toward innovation. Both are needed to create the context for an organizational identity that balances improvement and innovation. In the next chapter, we will develop the third essential leadership practice: *change your field of perception*.

SBK High School: Creating Context

Creating context as a leadership practice is present in SBK High School. School leaders are excited by evidence that current practice is being referenced against the urgency facing education as a whole and the district in particular. Several years ago, homework practices were being questioned and beliefs were being challenged. Work being done nationally through Ken O'Connor (2009), Rick Stiggins, Judith Arter, Jan Chappuis, and Stephen (2006), Doug Reeves (2001), and others related to assessing student work was brought into the local collaborative conversations. The work of the national experts was referenced to local practice. The conversations around this were polite, and some produced some movement to improve practice. As the context of addressing the future needs of the learner has become a part of the school identity, the momentum to look at grading practices has markedly increased. Although these conversations have been contentious at times, the purpose is always present: What is the evidence of student learning and how is it communicated? There is now constant referencing to the purpose of assessments, grades, homework, and instructional practices.

Staff is encouraged to make their homework practice public, and there is evidence that there is a shift in thinking and practice from more punitive to more encouraging. Purpose is seen in these statements; the emphasis on feedback and achievement is present. Staff is piloting standards-based grading as a way to more accurately report student progress.

Conversations are different now than they were a few years ago. The identity of this school as being excellent in academics and athletics is clear. However, it is now in the process of adapting to the learning needs of the students of the 21st century. The learning needs of students are being referenced to current practice. This has helped set the tone as leaders in this district create the context for making sense of what is being learned about the learner who will graduate 10 years from now. The culture of the school is slowly shifting and evolving.

TEAM CONVERSATION STARTERS

As a team, take the time to dialogue about your answers to the self-assessment from this chapter. Share your responses with one another, and begin to ascertain what your observations mean for your organization. What should you do about this?

Self-Assessment

Create Context

For this self-assessment, we ask you to consider what you value as you work to create context. Go through these concepts once making a mark for where you balance them in your work as a leader. Go through a second time and make a different mark for where your organization as a whole balances them. What differences, if any, do you notice? What does this difference mean for you and your organization?

Preserving identity	◆—◆—◆—◆—◆—◆	Evolving identity
Policy and procedure	◆—◆—◆—◆—◆—◆	Purpose
Structure	◆ ◆—◆—◆—◆—◆	Freedom
Autonomy	◆—◆—◆—◆—◆—◆	Belonging
Past	◆—◆—◆—◆—◆—◆	Future
Rules	◆—◆—◆—◆—◆—◆	Practical knowledge
What people expect	◆—◆—◆—◆—◆—◆	More than expected
Ideas fitting identity	◆—◆—◆—◆—◆—◆	Identity fitting ideas

Change Your Field **8** of Perception

Although we try, transformation cannot be externally mandated or directed. It can only be provoked. Change in internal meaning, not change by external mandate, is the source and catalyst for living system transformation.

—Stephanie Pace Marshall,
author and educator

We need to find new ways of doing things. . . . To do things differently, we must learn to see things differently. . . . It is a matter of survival in the new world of business.

—John Seely Brown, cofounder of the
Institute for Research on Learning

We assess for two reasons: (1) to gather evidence to inform instructional decisions and (2) to encourage students to try to learn. Both purposes must be well served for schools to be effective.

—Rick Stiggins, author and
assessment expert

IN THIS CHAPTER

This chapter will develop the background for understanding the third essential leadership practice necessary for evolving organizations that balance improvement and innovation: *change your field of perception.* This practice is derived from the change element of information and the innovative attribute of amplification. To start the presentation, a brief background for the important role information plays in creating adaptation in the natural world will be developed. The important role it plays in each of our lives will follow. Following this, the continuum of leadership behavior as it relates to an organization's use of information will be presented. Additionally, you will be provided with opportunities to reflect about how your leadership behavior moves on this continuum. Finally, some practical tips for changing your field of perception to use information in ways that help you and your organization balance improvement and innovation will be offered.

THE IMPORTANCE OF INFORMATION

When we speak of *information, we are referring to any input that causes a system to respond and create meaning.* For school leaders, this can be pending legislation, a report, student performance data, or new initiatives but also, and perhaps more important, includes things like a comment, an article, a conversation, a note from a child, a tear, or a smile. Information is any input that catches the attention of someone in the organization.

The Importance of Information in the Natural World

Earlier, the case was made that information is vital to the change process, including it as one of the change elements. In nature, change is constant, and information plays a central role in adaptation and survival. Packard states, "Survival has to do with gathering information about the environment, and responding appropriately" (Packard quoted in Lewin, 1999, p. 138). At all levels, from the cellular level to the complex workings of the human brain—and even to our organizations—systems rely on processing information to survive.

When we think of responding to information, there is a tendency to think of it as the gathering of facts to make decisions. We gather it by reading, listening, and watching—we organize it on our cell phones and PDAs, and we want quicker access to it through high-speed Internet connections and faster processors on our computers. In this mind-set, we think of information as informing us—in nature, the emphasis is on forming.

The word information is based on the verb *inform.* This verb comes from the Latin word *informare, meaning to give form to.* This is precisely how information works in the natural world: "Life uses information to organize matter into form, resulting in all the physical structures we see" (Wheatley, 1999b, p. 96).

In nature, forming is a response to newness—new, novel, information. "The source of life is new information—novelty—ordered into new structures" (Wheatley, 1999b, p. 96). Adaptation occurs in environments where lots of new information is created. New information is most abundant when systems are perturbed—when they move far from equilibrium toward a state of chaos. These are times when natural systems create new forms by reacting to unfamiliar information.

Zohar (1997) refers to the work of biologist Walter Freeman in citing how these chaotic circumstances provide information that leads to new forms and structures. Freeman studied the role chaos plays in the development of rabbits' sense of smell. What he found was that as rabbits encounter familiar smells, the information is quickly processed through existing neural wiring. However, when unfamiliar smells are encountered, "the nerve endings fire irregularly across all possible frequencies and amplitudes, poised to respond quickly to any change in input. This chaotic state allows the olfactory bulb to rewire itself to deal with new information" (p. 79).

Although information serves as the input that creates stability by leading organisms to familiar responses, it is by processing unfamiliar inputs that healthier, adaptive organisms are created. So the real importance of information in relation to change is revealed in its role in creating the unfamiliar inputs that force organisms to develop new responses. This newness gives systems the stuff they need not only to survive in their environments but also to thrive in them.

The Importance of Information in Our Lives

Information fulfills this role of creating newness for each of us as well. As infants, we are inundated with new information, and our brains are constantly wiring all of it to create meaning. New tastes, new smells, new sounds, new words, new movements—from this newness, new forms emerge. Throughout our early development, we form who we are by creating meaning from new information. Infant brains are completely malleable, and their wiring forms around the cultural information they process.

In these developing years, children participate in life the same way natural systems do. Information is everywhere, and young children fully engage with it. They seek out and throw themselves into newness as they slide, roll, bounce, touch, and taste throughout their day. All to create the stimulating information needed to wire their brains. There are minimal boundaries between young children and information. Even mistakes are not mistakes; it is information from which they learn.

As adults, we value steady states over the childhood desire for turbulent excitement in every moment. We filter inputs as we engage in more rational processes for making meaning of information. We can manage information

> When information is tightly controlled, the natural process of information creating new form is extinguished.

and control our responses by this means. Much is gained through our ability to manage information, yet something is lost as well. What is lost is the ability to connect with information more freely, to use it more as a creative force—something more aligned to the natural relationship of information to forming.

Command-and-control organizations value steady states over turbulence as well. With this mind-set, too much or the wrong kind of information disrupts the status quo. This can create unwelcome disturbances, so leaders of traditional organizations strive to control information. It has even gotten to the point where information overflow has led some companies to create the role of chief information officer in an attempt to manage it. If the goal is to keep information from stirring things up, then it follows that it should be controlled at the top and be distributed on a need-to-know basis. As Wheatley (1999b) articulates, traditional organizations "have no desire to let information roam about promiscuously, procreating where it will, creating chaos. Management's task is to enforce control, to keep information contained, to pass it down in such a way that no newness occurs" (p. 97).

When information is tightly controlled, the natural process of information creating new form is extinguished. Controlling information can increase standardization and consistency, but it also makes it harder for people to acquire the information they need to create relevance for their work. In nature, rich environments create many unfamiliar signals that organisms must respond to with new forms. People are part of nature, and when information becomes a commodity shared begrudgingly, each individual loses some of his or her vitality—the vitality that comes from information sparking new responses and new meaning.

No natural system separates itself from free-flowing information—for if it does, it dies. When information is allowed to flow more freely through the organization, we move closer to the conditions that create adaptation in nature. Just as with natural systems, these are times when newness abounds. And when new information is referenced with a strong identity, this is when we can adapt and evolve our organizations—this is when information stimulates new forms.

TAKE A MOMENT

Think about your organization: What does it look like when information is controlled? When it is free flowing? How do people respond to each?

ESSENTIAL LEADERSHIP PRACTICE—CHANGE YOUR FIELD OF PERCEPTION

The third leadership practice for creating systems that balance improvement and innovation is to change your field of perception. This practice has to do with a leader's conscious, continuous effort to make new information flow more freely through the organization.

Systems theorists highlight the importance of feedback loops. Feedback is "essential to sustenance and growth. . . . All life thrives on feedback and dies without it" (Wheatley, 2005, p. 158). This is how systems adjust their relationship to the environment. New information interacts with the system, the system responds in some way, additional information is generated because of the response, and it is then fed back to the system in a repeating cycle of information-response-feedback. These loops fit into two categories: (1) regulatory and (2) amplifying. Think of regulatory as having a diminishing effect and amplifying as having an expanding effect.

Regulatory feedback serves the function of keeping the system in balance. An example often used as a metaphor for this type of feedback is the thermostat in a house. Its function is to raise or lower the temperature setting to regulate a comfortable heat throughout the house. It keeps the temperature from moving too far in either direction—diminishing the effect of change.

This type of feedback is used in organizations to keep a system on track for the goals that have been planned. If performance dips (i.e., student learning, profits, product quality) corrective steps are taken to get it back to predetermined levels of acceptance. The action is to prevent change from going too far astray. Regulatory feedback loops are directly related to stabilizing a system.

Amplifying feedback serves the function of compounding change in one direction. It amplifies a change instead of regulating it. Information in this type of loop increases as it moves through the system's networks of relationships. This feedback loop is associated with growth and change, not stability. To illustrate this type of feedback, think of how something becomes popular (or unpopular) through word of mouth. It might be a movie, a book, an idea, or a fashion statement, such as the length of a skirt or the width of a necktie. Its rise or fall is based not just on the review of critics (or parents) but on the feedback that amplifies its importance in one direction or the other. This type of feedback uses "information differently, not to regulate, but to notice something new and amplify it into messages that signal a need to change" (Wheatley, 1999b, p. 78).

Goerner (1999) and Wheatley (1999b) view regulatory feedback as being reinforced in organizations

> When information flows more freely through the organization, people interact differently with it.

through mechanistic thinking. In such mind-sets, regulation is needed to keep systems from going out of balance, and just as with a thermostat, information is used to maintain a stable state. These authors view amplifying feedback as being more closely aligned to self-organizing systems. Amplification of information and its meaning leads to disturbances, creating new information and making adaptive responses possible. Amplifying feedback loops in organizations are formed when leaders create the conditions for information and the meaning it generates to be amplified throughout the system's networks of relationships.

Once again, think back to Randy from Chapter 3. After deciding that they could not address Randy's learning needs with current practice, the teacher and principal began to search for ways to help him. Many things were considered, but one idea caught their attention because of its potential match to the school's sense of self. They began talking to others in their network of relationships about the idea. Its meaning changed as people added their information. The idea was amplified in these conversations and began signaling a way to approach Randy's needs. The teacher was then ready to take action and adapt her teaching methods to help Randy.

When we say the next essential leadership practice is to change your field of perception, we are *referring to changing your perception about information and feedback.* Instead of just viewing information as *informing* and using it to *regulate* the system—stabilizing it and keeping it on target for reaching predetermined goals—begin to think of it in relationship to *forming* new structures and *amplifying* meaning. In this way, information can become a signal for change.

Instead of needing to control information and dispensing it with preassigned meaning to those who need to know, be freer with it. When information flows more freely through the organization, people interact differently with it. Individuals can then choose to be disturbed in ways that leaders cannot predetermine. When disturbed, they begin to pick up the signals for change, create meaning with it, and amplify that meaning through networks of relationships. When this happens, something wonderful follows. The information creates organization. People who notice the amplified meaning organize around the information to generate a response. Adaptive responses become possible because the information generates new behavior, new form, and new structures. This is our hope for innovation—shifting our field of perception regarding information is essential to growing that hope.

TAKE A MOMENT

Can you think of a situation where people self-organized around information? What could you do to take better advantage of that dynamic?

The leadership practice change your field of perception follows from the change element of information and amplification—an attribute of innovation. This relationship is shown in Figure 8.1.

Figure 8.1 Leading for Innovation—Change Field of Perception

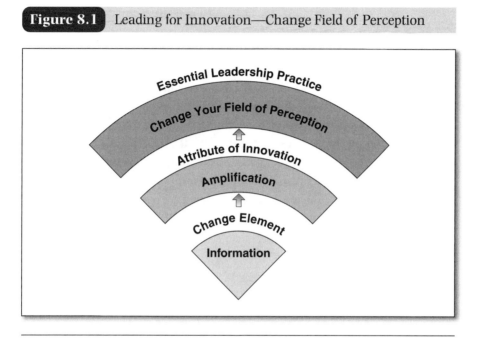

The Continuum of Leadership Behavior—Information

Although it is essential to the process of innovation to change the way one perceives information, we recognize that it is a counterintuitive shift for many educators. In today's schools, the information that is getting all the attention is in the form of student-performance data. The pressure of accountability creates a need to react quickly to student performance that is below accepted levels. In this atmosphere, mind-sets advocate close monitoring of student performance through frequent testing followed by prescriptive action. The thinking is that when performance is low it needs to be brought to an acceptable range as quickly as possible. This is like the thermostat in the room, and it naturally follows that such mind-sets use data to regulate student performance. Regulatory feedback loops are created, which when combined with a sense of urgency and threat, evolve a mental model that is largely unchallenged in schools—a mental model of student learning as something to be stabilized and regulated.

As authors, we understand the need for tracking student performance closely and responding to student learning needs to create successful learning for all. Our concern is that because of public perception and pressure, educational leaders have become too narrow in their focus regarding using student test data to regulate student learning. Keep in mind that the purpose of regulating feedback is to limit the effect of change—to keep it from going too far in one direction. So how can leaders help their systems look beyond current boundaries if test data are only used in regulating feedback loops?

At the heart of innovation is the need to understand information's role in generating novel form and structure. With amplifying feedback, it is possible to see things differently—to notice things we have not noticed that signal a need for change. Yet the underlying mind-set of command-and-control organizations values information's role in regulating and stabilizing systems. So a dilemma for educational leaders is to honor the value of information's role in regulating student performance while recognizing that innovation comes when information is used in amplifying feedback loops. To understand the spectrum of what leaders must deal with, we have created the leadership continuum for information.

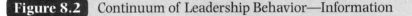

Figure 8.2   Continuum of Leadership Behavior—Information

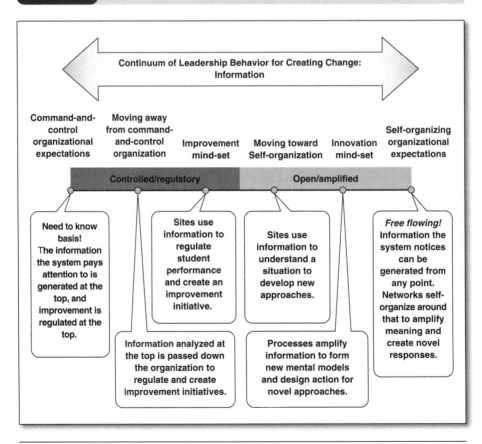

The continuum in Figure 8.2 represents the way information is viewed, from the command-and-control organization's sense of it needing to be controlled and used to regulate performance to the self-organizing view of information being important to forming new responses. That end of the spectrum reveals the need for information to be open and free flowing so that its role in creating new forms can be maximized.

Once again, the idea is for leaders to have a richer understanding of the full continuum so that they can use the most appropriate approach for the situation. Again, think back to the S-curve model. The growth stage of the curve is where improvement dominates. When improvement is the focus, information in regulatory feedback loops is important. Improvement is about getting better by setting goals and benchmarks and taking steps to reach these. Essential to this process is feedback that keeps a system on course. Knowing whether things are changing in a favorable or unfavorable direction is important here. It helps this process to interpret information frequently so that corrective measures can be designed and their effect analyzed. Systems use this to do more of the things that are working and less of the things that are not.

When systems need to move beyond current practice, such as at the introduction and maturity stages of the S-curve growth cycle, then information in regulatory feedback loops is not helpful. These feedback loops reinforce stability. At these times, disturbance is what leaders want to amplify so that change can occur. This is when amplifying feedback is needed. These relationships are shown in Figure 8.3.

Figure 8.3 Information and the S-curve

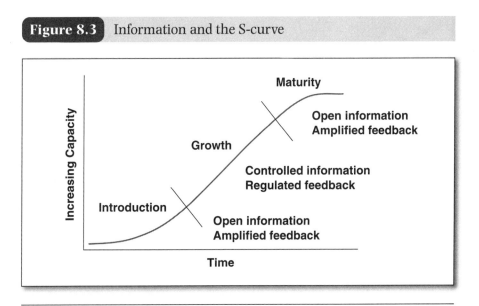

Teachers and administrators in today's schools work in environments where things are not simply *either-or* nor *black and white*. In reality, complexities about the role of information create contradictory messages in schools. On one hand, there is a strong tide in the direction of using information to monitor and regulate student learning. Most schools are involved in developing improvement plans in response to their district's directives to improve student performance in relationship to standards attainment. These plans focus on bringing performance in line with targeted goals. The way to achieve this usually involves testing of subskills, analysis of performance, corrective action, and retesting to begin the cycle anew. The basis of this use of information is rooted in regulatory feedback.

At the same time, there is a strong movement across the country, and globally, to use effective assessment as a means to improve student learning. At the heart of this movement is an expectation that students interpret and create personal meaning for what the assessment information is telling them about their learning. To do this, students are encouraged to interact with others and reflect on what they have to do to maximize their learning. In essence, students are expected to amplify the meaning of the information to generate adaptive responses. At the heart of this assessment movement is the use of information in amplifying feedback loops.

The point is that current movements in education are expecting teachers and administrators to move in opposite directions at the same time. These movements use two different approaches to information. The assessment movement will not work with mind-sets based in regulatory feedback. It is also likely that leaders using only information in amplifying feedback loops will be seen as ineffective in a system where regulatory feedback dominates. Unless a deeper understanding of the continuum of leadership expectations for information is developed, we cannot possibly hope to have leaders capable of leading for improvement and innovation.

WHAT CHANGING YOUR FIELD OF PERCEPTION LOOKS LIKE IN PRACTICE

As we look to leaders to understand how they apply their perception of information to their work, we find that it is difficult to isolate leaders' views of information from their perception of the two previous leadership practices: embrace dissonance and create context. We find that leaders who seek stability and rely on traditional approaches to create context see information as something to be controlled, and they use it in its regulatory function. Leaders who are open to disturbance and actively develop shared purpose see information as giving life to their system.

The life-giving part of information lies in its newness. Newness comes from information not being able to be confirmed with current patterns. When information is different, it gets noticed. So when leaders perceive dissonance as an ally, they are more likely to want information to flow around and interact with people. They intuitively understand that when information is freer someone may notice something new and different about it, thereby sparking a disturbance.

The leaders we notice who use both types of feedback recognize that when context is clear, information does not need to be tightly controlled. Instead of trying to create meaning for information and then sharing the meaning with people, these leaders try to be freer with information. They are inclined to trust people to create meaning to the information by combining it with a clearly understood, common purpose. In this combination of freedom and structure, the information is more likely to be noticed, be amplified, have its meaning evolve, and have an adaptive response emerge.

We find that leaders who lead for improvement and innovation consciously increase the flow of information in their organizations. They do this by first creating many ways for people to interact and build relationships. They believe that information means different things to each person, so they are more likely to resist the temptation to interpret it and then to tell people the meaning they have created. Rather, they encourage people to interact and interpret the information for themselves, creating ownership and empowerment. They do this by encouraging people to observe, notice, and wonder about what they see and think and then talk to and share their observations with others. In essence, these leaders view information as something to be owned by everyone, not something to be hoarded by those on top. Purpose, relationships, and information combine to create a powerful formula for transforming their systems.

More and more companies that rely on innovative thought are changing the way purpose, relationships, and information interact in their organizations. An example of this is Google, which has been cited as being at the top of the list of best places to work in America (Great Place to Work Institute, 2008). At the heart of this distinction is a different way of setting people up for work. Google creates organizational structures that encourage collaboration and creative freedom. Some of the things they do to increase the flow of information within these structures is to use surveys to solicit input (which are published for all to read); use in-house blogs so employees can share stories, notes, and updates on their work; have whiteboards all around the work environment so employees can start and add to discussions about things they notice; and have suggestion boxes if employees would rather give their input in this manner.

Google also attempts to design workspaces that are conducive to inter-action. They create attractive hallways and encourage people to interact there. The company encourages cross-function interactions in lunch-rooms, social gatherings, and recreational activities so new connections are developed. Management has an open-door policy and encourages any employee to speak out about concerns to any manager. Weekly gatherings are held that are Webcast to all their offices around the world. As part of these meetings, employees are encouraged to ask any question in an open forum. According to the Great Place to Work Institute (2008), Google is a company that realizes that a culture of collaboration and freely flowing information is the key to their growth, innovation, and success.

Organizations such as Google think that it is more important for infor-mation to create organization rather than the organization to create infor-mation. This is a mind-set common to the leaders we observe who are developing organizations that both improve and innovate. Imagine a sys-tem that possesses a well-articulated, common purpose. As information flows freely through such a system, people are free to notice it. And as they do, they seek out others to interpret it and create meaning. When the meaning grows strong enough, people organize around that. Those that are moved by the newness of the information come together to do some-thing about it—take action—to create something new. Once something is accomplished, this group dissolves. When moved again by information, another group forms with a different configuration of people to accom-plish another goal.

TAKE A MOMENT

In what ways do you currently have people interact with new information? What affect does this interaction have on deci-sion making? Would you want to do anything differently to increase this flow of new information and people's interac-tion with it?

Increasing Your Ability to Change Your Field of Perception

To work toward integrating the behaviors on the Continuum of Leadership Behavior for Creating Change, it is time to ask, what will it take to help you change the way you perceive information and feedback? What will it take for you to balance both controlling information and being more open with it? What will help you use both regulating feed-back loops and amplifying feedback loops? Once again, let us start by taking some time to consider several courageous conversation starters. To do this, go back to that reflective spot, take some time (once again) for that long walk in a private place, or revisit your reflective journal—it is time to consider the following:

- How does your organization use information to regulate? What structures help that? What structures get in the way of that? How does it use information to amplify? What processes help that? What processes get in the way of that?
- When, if ever, do you consciously move to the open/amplified side of the continuum? What does it feel like? How do others respond when you are there?
- What means do you use now to connect people across your organization? Are their things that get in the way of that? What could you do to minimize that? What could you do to create new connections?
- Imagine creating the type of organization where people self-organize around important issues and good things happen for kids as a result. What did you do to create that type of organization?

ACTION TIPS—CHANGE YOUR FIELD OF PERCEPTION

Following are some tips for helping you become more comfortable with our second essential leadership practice: change your field of perception.

See Information as Nourishment

Organisms use information to stay in sync with their environments. The most adaptive systems in nature thrive when information is abundant. Information is a life-giving force for these systems. It can be a life-giving force for organizations as well. Yet here, leaders think their role is to control information and protect people from the burden of processing it. When they do, they fail to capitalize on its life-giving properties.

People in schools are hungry for meaningful information and for the opportunity to collaborate with others. Nourish them. You do not have to generate information to do this. It is already present in your organization. Start to nourish your system by giving people the opportunity to interact with one another. When they do, their information interacts. New information is generated every time this happens. More important, people naturally look to one another to create meaning. As meaning develops, new information is generated and others use their information to interact with it. In this way, it renews itself and starts to flow through webs of relationships.

Webs of information are more meaningful to people than the official channels of communication. Actually, these webs already exist in your school organization. They are how gossip and rumor circulate. Why not use them to create a healthy system by allowing meaningful information to circulate through them?

Continually make sure that the context of people's work is always clear and widely understood, and then get people together. Learn from Google and other innovative companies to make information more transparent, more open. You don't have to be overt and declare that you are starting a new information initiative. Just work on that shared purpose, get people together, make information more open and visible, and then get out of the way.

You can expect some messes, as this is the nature of information: to create bursts of chaos. But take heart, it is a sign that your school organization is alive. Have fun with the messes, they are only temporary—they signal that a deeper understand is about to follow. Think of information as nourishment—help it become abundant. It is what people need to understand their role in the school environment.

Remember That Information Forms

Nature offers us powerful images for how transformative change occurs. Systems naturally transform without a strategic plan or a directive from the superintendent. Earlier, we said that it is more important for information to create organization than it is for the organization to create information. What we hope to create with that statement is a picture in your mind of information being a catalyst for transformation in organizations, just as it is in nature. We hope to create an image of people coming forward and self-organizing around information. In our statement, we are not saying that organizations should not produce information. Of course, they should; it is an important function of survival. However, this is not the catalyst for transformation. If we want innovation as well as improvement, then we need to do our best to replicate how transformational change happens in nature.

To do this, we need to give people the opportunity to notice new things and to be disturbed about what this information means in relationship to the common purpose. We need them to process this information by creating meaning for it. They need to feed that information into their networks. As that meaning grows and changes, we need to give people the freedom to do something about it. To organize around and take action in a way that brings life to the shared purpose. When leaders create a meaningful context and issue fewer directives, they tap into the power of people to organize around information and to respond to it by creating new ideas, new practice, and new form. This is a resource for deep change that most school organizations have yet to use well. Start by visualizing information as the catalyst for bringing people together. Good things will follow.

The Little Blips Generate More Leverage Than the Big Chunks

When we talk to leaders about innovation, repeatedly, they mention how an innovation got started with something small, such as a comment, a word, or a chance conversation. We never hear them speak about innovation following because of a large-scale initiative. We speculate that this is because when the initial, small bit of information disturbs us, it is not threatening. It is as if by its small size we are given the opportunity to consider it in a playful, unthreatening way. This sparks curiosity, wonder, and creativity.

It also seems that the small bits catch us off guard and nudge us without causing a defensive reaction. Little bits of information can spread quickly through our neural networks. These bits may produce no reaction, or they may spark a connection that grows into a meaningful idea. Large initiatives come loaded with detail. They do not pass quickly through our neural networks. We analyze them and break things down to understand what it means. Because of their size, they may even trigger resistance. Most significant, they may be too dense to spark the kinds of connections that grow into innovation.

Give the people in your school organization lots of opportunities to talk about the things they are noticing. Have them connect in ways that they may not ordinarily have a chance to. Encourage cross function interaction. Do so in a way that is natural, relaxed, and low on stress. This gives opportunities for little bits of information to interact and spark something of significance.

PARADOXICAL LEADERS

It may be hard to think of something more paradoxical than controlling something while letting it be free. Yet that is exactly what we are asking leaders to do with information. Innovation will not follow when information is only used to regulate. An innovative organization needs to use information in the same way adaptive systems do in nature. This can only happen when amplifying feedback loops are encouraged. At the same time, leaders cannot ignore the importance regulatory information has to educational systems today. This is the reality leaders work in. To create vital systems that improve and innovate, leaders need to be able to do both: use information to regulate and use it to amplify into adaptive responses.

To help you integrate the concepts of regulating *and* amplifying information into a cohesive whole, it is important for you to start by becoming limber in moving across the continuum. To create the context for developing a leadership practice that unifies both, we invite you to integrate the following paradoxical statement into your job description: Use information to inform and to form.

Use Information to Inform and to Form

To help start your journey to achieving a healthy balance between using information to inform and to form, reflect on the following:

- How would you describe the balance between using information to inform and to form at this time? If a healthier balance is needed, what first step might you take toward that?
- What might you do to help others in your organization develop greater clarity about information and its role in regulating and amplifying?
- In your personal life, how do you use information and regulatory loops? How do you use information and amplifying loops? Is there anything you would do differently with this understanding?

SUMMARY

The third of our essential leadership practices for leading for improvement and innovation is change your field of perception. This practice evolves from the change element of information and the innovative attribute of amplification. In nature, systems and organisms have an open relationship with information in their environment. To these systems, information's essential role is to create new forms and structures. This happens when disruptive information is processed in amplifying feedback loops.

Organizations filter and control information in attempts to maintain stability. This keeps information from creating disturbances and messes in organizations. It also creates a tendency for the use of information in regulatory feedback loops only. These loops are useful for steering toward and assessing progress toward predetermined goals, but they stifle the development of innovative, adaptive approaches. Information in amplifying loops is what is needed for the emergence of these approaches.

This chapter advocates for leaders to change their field of perception regarding information. Leaders are asked to understand how information in amplifying feedback creates adaptive change. Leaders are also encouraged to create the conditions for the growth of these loops in their school organizations by connecting people across the organization in new ways. Additionally, leaders are asked to encourage people to notice new things, to talk to others about what they see, and to create meaning together. Finally, leaders are encouraged to give people the freedom to create adaptive responses within the context of the shared purpose. Leaders need to become aware of using information in both types of feedback loops. Both are needed to help systems balance improvement and innovation. In the next chapter, we will develop the fourth essential leadership practice: *let ideas collide.*

SBK High School: Changing Field of Perception

The leadership practice of shifting perception through using information to amplify ideas is becoming a reality in SBK High School and its supporting districts. In the process of learning about the urgency facing education and coming to understand the learning needs of the 21st-century learner, information is shared through the efforts of the 60-member group. In the first session, participants learned about the sense of urgency by participating in a videoconference with David Warlick, national speaker and author of *Raw Materials for the Mind and Redefining Literacy for the 21st Century.* One of the participants was skeptical and stated that he could not believe this was really happening with *our students* and in *our schools.* He grew increasingly uncomfortable with what he heard and chose to express it to those who would listen.

The second session focused on the global economy and the changing business scene. That information expanded the learning of all, but particularly educators. Some people expressed concern about the creating jobs for dropouts or graduates who were "nonschool students." The panel responded that those jobs do not exist in this global economy in this country.

The focus of the third session was on "learning from the learner." In preparation, each participant of the group was encouraged to interview at least three students and post their findings on a blog that had been created. The person referenced earlier asked that several students be made available to him at the high school so that he could interview them. By the time this individual finished with these student conversations, he became more informed about the realities of student learning. At the third session, participants learned from the student interviews posted on the blog and a video of actual students in the schools. During the synthesis process, the prior skeptic was an active, enthusiastic, enlightened contributor sharing what he had learned from the students.

The leaders in this initiative have shifted their perception of their leadership practice from providing information or directing participants on what to think to providing opportunities to make meaning of what participants were learning. They provided some structure with the freedom to make sense of what is being learned. As a result, rich dialogue is taking place, ideas are being amplified, and mental models are being revealed.

TEAM CONVERSATION STARTERS

As a team, take the time to engage in a dialogue around the following:

- How does our organization deal with newness currently?
- Are ideas well formed before people work with them? Or are people encouraged to interact with incomplete ideas?
- What does our current use of information mean for our ability to innovate?
- What could we do differently?

Self-Assessment

Change Your Field of Perception

In this chapter, we have encouraged you to change your perception of information and the role it plays in not only informing but also in forming new order. To help you better visualize and understand your current perceptions—and to envision how you would like these perceptions to change—we offer the following self-assessment. Below are eight concepts relevant to the role information plays in leadership. Write these terms into the quadrants that describe where you are currently at regarding your ability to use them and the importance they have for your leadership. Then use a different color to write them in for where you would like these concepts to be in your use and leadership. Reflect about the differences you observe and what they suggest for your growth as a leader.

Regulating feedback	Amplifying feedback
Organization creates information	Information creates organization
Need to know basis	Free flowing
Work with complete ideas	Work with incomplete ideas

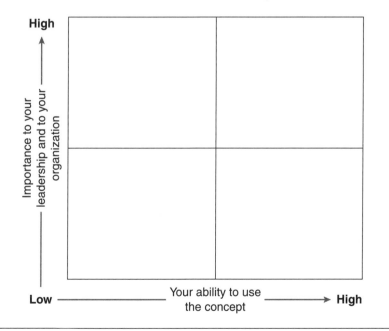

Let Ideas Collide

Innovation events occur when new ideas are tried; innovative culture occurs when new ideas become ingrained in the way work is done.

—Dave Ulrich, author and professor

Order emerges at the edge of chaos. . . . The order that arises is not imposed by central design; it derives from distributed influence through the interactions of the system's agents.

—Roger Lewin and Birute Regine, authors and consultants

IN THIS CHAPTER

This chapter will develop the background for understanding the fourth essential leadership practice necessary for evolving organizations that balance improvement and innovation: *let ideas collide.* This practice is derived from the change element of order and the innovative attribute of engagement. To start the presentation, a brief background for the concept of order and the role it plays in creating adaptation in the natural world will be developed. The important role it plays in each of our lives will follow. The continuum of leadership behavior as it relates to an organization's means of creating order will be presented. Once again, you will be provided with opportunities to reflect on how your leadership behavior moves on this continuum. Finally, some practical tips for developing the leadership practice let ideas collide will be offered so that you can create the conditions that help you and your organization balance improvement and innovation.

THE IMPORTANCE OF ORDER

In the previous chapter, we spoke about how new information stimulates new responses. The whole idea of a system being open to new information and dissonance as a catalyst for creating new responses is so that the most important of those responses can become the new way of doing things. This process allows the system to adjust and adapt, to remain current and in sync with its environment. What we want to bring forward in this chapter is how this adaptive action creates new order. It is not enough for systems to generate new responses. The new responses must lead to a new way of being or behaving. A new order must continuously be created by the system without losing its overall stability.

When we speak of *order, we are speaking of what holds a system together*. In both the natural world and in organizations, creating order is about generating structures that create the stability that allows a system to maintain itself while also allowing it to adapt to changes so that it remains in sync with its environment.

The Importance of Order in the Natural World

For many years, science taught that order and disorder were opposing forces. Most of us rely heavily on derivatives of these perceptions in our lives. We seek order and abhor disorder. Today, science is telling us a different story; in the natural world, order and disorder are not antagonists but allies. They work together in systems to create a paradoxical state of dynamic stability. The surprising message in all this is that systems use disorder to adapt and create greater order: They remain stable by constantly changing.

The fact the disorder is needed to produce greater order may be hard to grasp at first. It was hard at first for scientists as well. Previously, science thought that, over time, systems wound down, losing energy, and eventually, they came to a state of rest or even death. This led to a belief that order needs to be imposed by a constant outside force to keep a system from winding down. The concept of constantly imposed order ruled science and influenced thinking in other areas for 300 years. The belief that organizations are machines in need of constant command by leaders is a direct derivative of this.

Science now tells us that order forms very differently in natural systems. Rather than losing energy while winding down, systems use an influx of energy through the system to force more order. An influx of new energy encourages a system to relinquish its present structural form so that it can reorganize in a way that allows it to remain in sync with its environment. This process allows old order to be replaced with new order while a system maintains stability. So the important point for leaders to consider is that science now tells us that order forms from a system's internal dynamics; it does not need to be imposed by an outside force.

Natural systems continuously reorder by using a process of dynamic interaction. When we use the term *dynamic interaction, we mean the process where the individual entities that make up the system interact with a constant influx of newness.* They participate with information in a dynamic process that leads to reordering.

The process works like this: Newness is outside of current order; therefore, when it presents itself, disorder is introduced into the system. Individual entities create potential energy in the form of meaning for this new information then spread it throughout the system. In the networks, the meaning of the new information grows; changes; and eventually, if it is important enough, engages the existing order. The important concept here is the engagement of current order.

Engagement is the stage where the meaning of a new idea has grown in strength and must engage the current order. Think of it as the youthful bighorn ram in the mountains that challenges the head of the herd for dominance. They charge toward each other with horns lowered and collide with a great force. Eventually, one wins; new order comes to the herd, or old order is retained. This description can serve as a metaphor for what we mean by the relationship of engagement and order. The violent impact is not what we want you to recall; we want you to recall how something new must eventually confront existing order and win or fade into the background. If the newness must be accounted for, the system reorders itself to it. If the newness is not important, then current order prevails. This is how systems reorder from dynamic interaction.

The Importance of Order in Our Lives

Order through dynamic interaction is behind how we develop knowledge and stimulate creative endeavors. Think of how the body of knowledge in the medical field develops, whether it's with the flu or with an organ transplant. There is a constant influx of information into the field about new medicines, new research, and new technologies. Old ideas must be dissipated and replaced by new ideas to maintain stability. Networks of doctors and medical

> Old ideas must be dissipated and replaced by new ideas to maintain stability.

professionals interact with this information. Each person creates meaning in his or her work and shares that meaning in his or her networks. Eventually, the ideas generated grow in importance and engage the existing order of practice. If the ideas are better, old order is replaced by new order. Through doctors and medical professionals actively interacting with new information, the knowledge in the field of medicine is constantly changing, yet overall, it remains predictable and stable. The overall stability means that you can still count on your doctor to help you heal.

Dynamic interaction is also an important component of creativity. Professionals who count on newness the most, those in fields such as design, marketing, new product development, research, and the arts, seek to inject newness into their work. They do this to generate large amounts of new information. They stimulate their environment with bits and scraps of information, phrases, pictures, sketches, textures, and wonder. The new information bounces around and collides with other ideas constantly. The intent is to create unpredictability so that a new spark can grow into the next important idea. Think back to Chapter 2 and the adaptive challenge George Lucas presented to his film crew. In these situations, professionals capitalize on dynamic interaction by creating newness to stimulate diversity, creativity, adaptation, and long-term stability—just as systems in nature do.

In short, order is about replacing old ways with new ways without having everything fall apart. Ordering and reordering are products of dynamic interaction in our lives as well as in nature. The important point to note is that reordering develops from participating with information rather than from an imposed force.

In our organizations, it is even more difficult than in our personal lives to perceive order as emerging from a process of dynamic participation with information rather than from an imposed force. Our organizations are built on views of order derived from an old science perspective where order and disorder cannot coexist. In this view, predictability, reliability, and control are associated with order. One of the manifestations of this thinking is a mental model that order will not happen without the imposed force of top management.

Current efforts to help schools adapt new ways come from perceptions that students do not possess the reading, mathematics, and technological skills needed in the workforce and that, overall, students are achieving below expectations. These perceptions are a signal to many people that public education has become disorderly and that order needs to be restored. In this mind-set, the presence of disorder creates a response to impose order from an outside source. Well-intended legislators and public leaders try to make things right by imposing legislation and mandates from the political arena. In response to laws and acts designed to reestablish order, local systems generate initiatives from the top. These initiatives are often characterized by step-by-step planning with corresponding controls to regulate progress.

If we expect our educational systems to be responsive to changes in the external environment, we must help leaders move away from practices based on the idea that order comes only when imposed from the top. Such practices are suited to creating predictability—they are not suited to creating adaptation. Leadership practices based in a perception of order being a process of continuous reordering through dynamic interaction are better suited to creating adaptive systems.

TAKE A MOMENT

What practices/initiatives are currently driving your school or district that come from formal leadership? What impact are these changes having on improved student achievement? Are these changes enough to bring all students to success? Do others who are not in a formal leadership positions also have ideas that might contribute to successful student learning?

How does the organization respond to all these ideas?

ESSENTIAL LEADERSHIP PRACTICE—LET IDEAS COLLIDE

The fourth leadership practice for creating systems that balance improvement and innovation is to let ideas collide. This leadership practice is about creating the conditions for new responses to become the new norm—for the old ways to be replaced by new ways. It is about recognizing reordering as something that emerges from supporting conditions rather than an imposed will. Adaptation cannot be imposed in nature, nor can it be achieved in our schools through legislation and mandate. Adaptation is about reordering to remain in sync with the environment, and reordering emerges when ideas collide, grow in importance, and interact with the existing order. It occurs in organizations when people are dynamically interacting with ideas and reordering around their meaning.

The conditions for adaptation are created by the practices we have been describing in previous chapters. It happens when new information can generate dissonance and when new ideas emerge from this process. The meaning of the new ideas amplifies when referenced against a context that authentically relates to a shared purpose. Once new ideas grow in strength, the most important ones need to become a part of what holds the system together—a part of the system's new order. The way this happens is when ideas collide and compete with other ideas. They bang into one another, change, and create new information and new meaning. If the emerging ideas are strong enough, the old ways dissipate and are replaced by the new ideas. This then sparks a new relationship to other ideas, and a new order is formed.

In Randy's story from Chapter 3, the reordering stage occurred after new techniques were tried with Randy and results were seen. These results were shared with others around the school district. As the meaning of the results grew, the district could not ignore what had been accomplished with Randy. The new practice engaged the existing order, and because it was important, the district reordered around the new information.

The leadership practice *let ideas collide* reminds leaders to encourage dynamic interaction. In schools, dynamic interaction happens when leaders create the conditions where people can do meaningful work together. Ideas collide when teachers share their understanding, discover one another's thinking, and together develop a deeper understanding of the practices that really work for students. This collision of ideas leads to reordering when the new understandings can openly engage existing practice—and there is openness to finding better ways. This is what we expect of our medical, optometry, or dental professionals. Think of how the standard for vision correction has moved from glasses, to contact lenses, to refractive vision correction procedures. This reordering and openness is what we should expect from the profession of education as well.

TAKE A MOMENT

Reflect on a situation in your classroom or school where new ideas emerged when people worked together and something new was created as a result.

What conditions were present that fostered these results?

The leadership practice let ideas collide follows from the change element of order and the attribute of innovation—engagement. This relationship is shown in Figure 9.1.

Figure 9.1   Leading for Innovation—Engagement

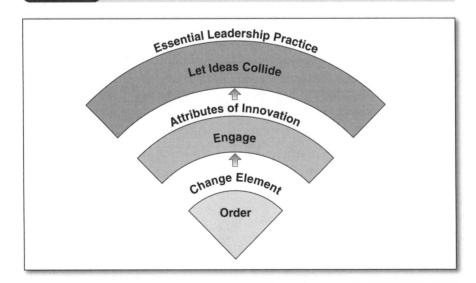

The Continuum of Leadership Behavior—Order

Throughout this book, we have been saying that innovation is about bringing forth something new. Traditional organizational expectations view order as being predictable and reliable and that the absence of these is disorder. So they approach creating something new in ways that are controlled and tightly planned. Dynamic interaction is the process that creates adaptive systems. Conversely, this process uses disorder to drive reordering. Therefore, to create innovation, the leader's role is not to impose order but to create the conditions for new order to emerge.

The leadership practice of let ideas collide honors the way reordering occurs in nature and in important aspects of our lives, but it runs counter to the traditional view of order where the leader is expected to impose order. Leaders leading for improvement and innovation are faced with honoring the traditional view of order valued by organizations while recognizing that meaningful reordering forms from ideas colliding to create a dynamic interaction of new and

Figure 9.2 Continuum of Leadership Behavior—Order

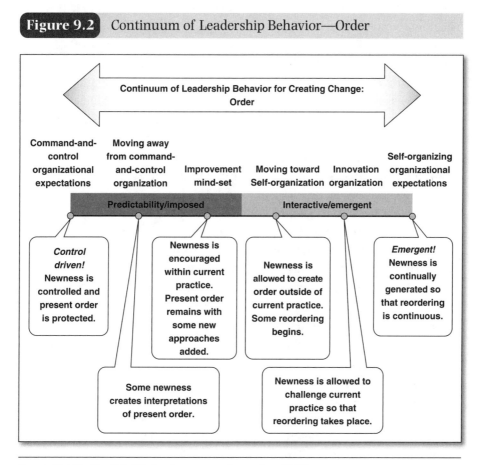

old ways. To understand the spectrum of what leaders must deal with, we have created the leadership continuum for order (Figure 9.2).

Welcoming Newness

How organizations treat newness helps reveal underlying beliefs about order and reordering. Newness left to move about an organization at will presents problems for school leaders with traditional mind-sets. Newness creates messes and unpredictability because it does not have a place to fit with present order. This causes problems for leaders who see it as their responsibility to protect against disorder. To these leaders newness should be dealt with cautiously because it is unpredictable and does not have a body of evidence that allows leaders to know how it will perform on the large scale.

Improvement mind-sets recognize that new ideas are necessary. Yet still rooted in traditional views of order, newness in improvement mind-sets tends to be subject to controls and regulation so as not to create disorder in the system. Improvement initiatives tend to desire newness that adds to the present order, not newness that engages the present order leading to reordering.

An innovation mind-set recognizes that new forms beyond current practice need to be developed. So in this mode, leaders tend to recognize that newness needs to perturb and replace current practice in a way that challenges present order. Leaders here are trying to use new ideas to break apart old ways, not add to them. These leaders perceive their organization as actively searching for change yet stable on the large scale.

The challenge for those leading for improvement and innovation is to have a richer understanding of the full continuum so that they can use both views of order, predictability and emergent, as appropriate. Once again, think back to the S-curve model. The growth stage of the curve is where improvement mind-sets can be productive. When improvement is the focus, determining the reliability and predictability of ideas is important. This is the time for ideas that are working to be widely instituted. To do that, it is necessary to expect the practice to be universally applied across the system. To accomplish this, it is important to plan how the practice will be learned and implemented. Planning in this way is a means of imposing order. So at these times, leaders need to honor the traits of the predictability/imposed side of the continuum.

When systems need to move beyond current practice, such as at the introduction and maturity stages of the S-curve growth cycle, order needs to be honored for its emergent capabilities, and imposed order needs to fade into the background. Newness needs to be amplified and encouraged so that emerging forms challenge existing practice. At these times, dynamic interaction leads to strengthening the system through reordering. This is when the system adjusts to changes in the environment without falling completely apart. Imposed order does not create the adaptive behavior necessary at these stages. Dynamic interaction does. These relationships are shown in Figure 9.3.

Figure 9.3   Order and the S-Curve

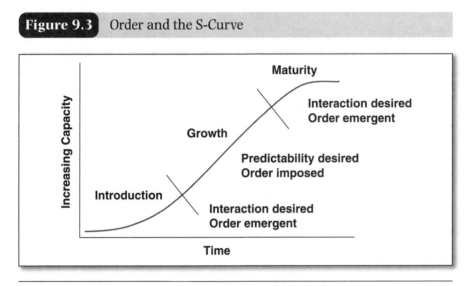

As we discussed in the previous chapter, teachers and administrators in today's schools work in environments where things are not as clearly delineated as the preceding description might suggest. In reality, this is a time when the thinking about how to create order can be rather muddied and contradictory. On one hand, there is a strong force in the direction of imposing regulations to drive student learning to levels associated with orderly, predictable systems. The culture of high stakes testing was conceived with this force. Initiatives such as this stem from a belief that order is achieved by imposing the learning structure and standardizing outputs. It is believed that in the absence of these structures there will be too much variation in performance, a sign used to cite the system as being disorderly. The thinking is that without such imposed order the overall system of education will be incapable of bettering itself and will become increasingly disorderly.

On the other hand, there are initiatives to put instructional decisions in the hands of local leaders, teachers, and students. Assessment *for* Learning can again be used to represent this type of thinking. This approach sees learning as a continuous reordering process. Learning in this perspective is an individual meaning-making process and is enhanced when people take charge of their learning and make adjustments based on performance information feedback. In this view, learning is a personal reordering process.

Current movements in education are expecting teachers and administrators to create order in opposing ways. The high-stakes testing movement does not mesh with a belief that learning is a personal reordering process. The assessment movement will not work with mind-sets based on the belief that learning works best when an outside force imposes order. Unless leaders understand the implications present in the two mental models of order, we cannot possibly expect them to lead for improvement and innovation.

WHAT LETTING IDEAS COLLIDE LOOKS LIKE IN PRACTICE

> Mixing ideas together, letting them interact and bounce around, creates varied levels of volatility.

When leaders perceive order and disorder to be part of a dynamic meaning-making process—where disorder precedes the development of more order—they see their responsibility as creating the conditions for order to form. This view perceives order as an interactive process based on individuals making meaning of new ideas and creating shared meaning, which leads to reordering present practice.

The leaders we work with that balance improvement and innovation understand that imposed order comes with a downside. They believe that too many directives limit people's ability to create. We also find that these leaders demonstrate an understanding that order does not form randomly; they recognize that allowing order to form from dynamic interaction is not a matter of anything goes. These leaders are conscious of creating a mix of structure and freedom and that this combination changes based on the understanding of their staff and the surrounding conditions.

These leaders work hard to create structure through purpose rather than imposing it: Structure through purpose confines new ideas bouncing around. Mixing ideas together, letting them interact and bounce around, creates varied levels of volatility. So ideas colliding need to be held together, contained in some common reference, so that they can interact with one another and direct the energy toward a common purpose. The right "container" does not confine colliding ideas too tightly or too loosely. The leaders who do this well allow ideas to interact and collide, yet they do so in a way that thoughtfully engages present practice.

We find that leaders who are blending this into a culture that balances improvement and innovation understand that this involves a transition process where structure may be more directed at first. As people understand the container and get better at assimilating it, more freedom is given.

We also find that these leaders possess other important attributes. First, they inherently tend to understand nonlinearity. By this, we mean that they realize that cause and effect are not always directly connected or closely related in time. Their actions show some level of understanding that systems are complex and that they need to be understood in deeper ways. What this says to us is that they see systems as more than the sum of their parts.

Additionally, these leaders are not afraid to let incomplete ideas circulate through the organization. Often, they prefer this to having ideas be well groomed before introducing them to others. As a result, these leaders are willing to let a process move into unknown territory. They trust the container they have created, and they trust that the results of the process will be productive. They tolerate messes as long as they know they are confined within the organization's purpose.

We also notice that effective leaders actively support people in letting go of old ways. They understand that the process of letting go is unique for each person. It is sometimes difficult and often makes people feel vulnerable. This can produce a range of behavior from resistance, to fear, to avoidance. These leaders are conscious of this and work hard to understand where people are at so that they can provide the emotional support and encouragement needed to transition to new ways.

Others describe these leaders as knowing what they want and having high expectations. Their involvement is direct but not interfering. By this, people are saying that others know these leaders care and want to work closely with what is going on but that they do so with respect to the efforts of others. They trust people and respect the processes that have been created to get work

> A changed field of perception regarding information honors newness.

done. They listen, question, and continually reference the shared intent when they get feedback from others. These leaders are respected for their honesty and their commitment to wanting everyone they work with to give their best.

As one might expect, these leaders are working to integrate the other three leadership practices into their repertoire. Embracing dissonance opens a system to understanding that disturbances can lead to deeper order. Creating context becomes the container we have just described. A changed field of perception regarding information honors newness. When letting ideas collide is added to these practices, a synergy is created where the culture of the school or district is receptive to continuous reordering—where improvement and innovation coexist.

Increasing Your Ability to Let Ideas Collide

To work toward integrating the behaviors on the Continuum of Leadership Behavior for Order (Resource C), it is time to ask the following: What is your perception of how order forms? What steps will you take to balance imposing order and letting it emerge? Once again, let us start by taking some time to consider several courageous conversation starters. To do this, go back to that reflective spot, take some time for that long walk in a private place, or revisit your reflective journal—it is time to consider the following:

- Where on the continuum would you place your leadership behavior relative to order? Where would others place you? Why? What could you do to help others better understand a need for behavior to move across the continuum?
- How does your organization reorder? What structures encourage that? What structures get in the way of that? What processes help that? What processes get in the way of that?
- When, if ever, do you consciously move to the interactive/emergent side of the continuum? What does it feel like? How do others respond when you are there?
- How are you currently doing with balancing imposed order with letting order emerge through interaction? Are there things you would do to create a healthier balance? How ready are the people you work with to move from structure to freedom? What could you do to help them make such a move?
- Imagine that your organization has become a place where people continuously reorder their collective practice around important learning issues. How did you do that?

ACTION TIPS—LET IDEAS COLLIDE

Following are some tips for helping you become more comfortable with our fourth essential leadership practice: let ideas collide.

Order Will Emerge

Chaos theory, a field of science study, had a chance to evolve after the introduction of supercomputers. With this technology, scientists were able to plot the behavior of systems that seemed chaotic. Previously, when these behaviors were plotted over several hundred occurrences, they seemed random and without form. However, supercomputers allowed these behaviors to be plotted over millions of occurrences. When this was done, deep order was revealed in intricate and stunningly beautiful patterns. The humbling realization for scientists was that order is always present—it may be difficult to detect at times, but when the view is broad enough, order emerges.

We have found that this is a very important view to keep in mind for leaders. At times, all teams and individuals struggle as they wrestle with newness. Things become disorderly as old patterns are challenged by new approaches. No one likes this feeling, and people try to drive it out as soon as possible. This can cause groups and individuals to want to impose a solution to a problem quickly so that discomfort is replaced by action. When leaders remind themselves that order will emerge when things seem to be disorderly, it affords them patience and causes pause before taking the bull by the horns and imposing order. We recommend that you teach this to your staff or students. It allows everyone to step back and trust that even though things seem uncomfortable, it is a natural part of reordering. More patience can develop when people understand that disorder is not a spiral down to chaos; it is the beginning of new order. When people recognize that order is present but may not yet be evident, groups are more likely to let ideas collide—to dig deeper and search longer for solutions and approaches that go beyond current practice. We have found that people's whole demeanor changes when they trust that order will emerge. They become less anxious about creating a fix, more connected to one another, and more focused on reaching the common goal.

Think of Yourself as a Coach

Coaching has been widely incorporated by the private sector to enhance the productivity of managers and executives. It has also evolved to the level of personal coaching—where people receive individual support for improving aspects of their lives. "What has emerged is a profession that works with individual clients to help them achieve results and sustain life-changing behavior in their lives and careers" (Whitworth, Kimsey-House, & Sandhal, 1998, p. xi).

What makes a coaching relationship powerful is that, unlike mentoring, the coach does not impose a personal will or give advice to a coachee. The relationship is based on the coach helping the coachee clarify personal understandings and draw out sustainable action based on those emergent understandings. At the fundamental level, the coach is helping the coachee reorder. Through questions and reflection, the coach encourages the collision of thoughts and ideas so that the coachee's old patterns can break down and new ones can form. The object of coaching is to help the client become more capable. This is achieved through a process that parallels dynamic interaction.

We encourage you to become more familiar with the role of the coach—not so that you can become a personal coach to others but so you can incorporate a coach's mind-set into your everyday work. With this mind-set, rather than directing people, you can bring out the thinking of others so it can be clarified and nurtured into action, which strengthens accountability and dampens dependence. It creates a greater sense of potency that can spread throughout a school or district. People are more likely to stop seeing the leader as someone to please and more likely to see him or her as someone who leads. When a coaching mind-set becomes accessible to all your personal and team interactions, a culture of emergence develops—one where individuals in the organization are encouraged to evolve to levels of greater capacity.

Use a Devil's Advocate

Most meetings are guarded discussions where people weigh the right thing to say before putting ideas on the table. Meetings are usually not the place to take a devil's advocate position—that is, if you want to hold on to your job. A devil's advocate is a skeptic, someone who takes a contrary position for the sake of argument. Ordinarily, this is someone who is very unpopular at meetings. We find that a powerful approach to meetings involves the leader appointing someone to the role of devil's advocate before the meeting starts. For obvious reasons, it should be someone different each time, not a consistent individual. We have worked with leaders who have done this and experienced first-hand how this strategy changes the discussion.

The person in this role is encouraged to take the counter position as issues are discussed, with the intent of pointing out holes in plans, ideas, and thinking. This role also includes identifying unintended, unseen consequences to proposed actions. This puts issues on the table for all to interact with, issues that might otherwise be discussed in the parking lot after the meeting. With these issues on the table, the potential to move the conversation from discussion to dialogue is available and strengthened.

Many meetings are characterized as discussions where people try to assert their *rightness*. Adopting a devil's advocate moves rightness to the issues and away from the individuals. A devil's advocate also encourages diversity of opinion. We find that this also encourages the honoring of diversity throughout the organization as leaders leave the meetings and work with others. The colliding of ideas is richer with greater creative potential when they are diverse.

PARADOXICAL LEADERS

The power of a paradox is that it helps draw attention to the full range of elements associated with a concept. When leaders see their work in paradoxes, it stimulates efforts to blend diverse elements into a coherent whole, instead of keeping them as separate and incompatible. The blending of paradoxical elements is very important when it comes to a leader's ability to create order. This is because it is not healthy for organizations to have only imposed order or order forming independently. It is the blending of the two—and getting the combination right—that is the challenge for today's leaders. Order needs structure to form. Too much structure is stifling for those working in our educational systems. Not enough structure leads to incoherence.

Balancing improvement and innovation requires leadership that welcomes instability while preserving stability. Growth, creativity, and innovation come through the ability to balance stability with instability. Finding the optimum blend of these two forces is the journey of leadership.

To help you integrate the concepts of imposing order and letting it emerge, it is important for you to start becoming limber in moving across the continuum. To create the context for developing a leadership practice that unifies both, we invite you to integrate the following paradoxical statement into your job description: Use instability to strengthen stability.

Use Instability to Strengthen Stability

Including this in your job description emphasizes the importance of helping others not be afraid of newness and the disruption to the status quo that it may bring. Let newness lead to wonder—and let wonder lead to new understandings—and let new understandings lead to breaking down old order so new can form. Let all of this happen in a way that allows the things that should never change (i.e., vision, mission, purpose) to grow stronger, reorder, and adapt to new demands. To help start your journey to achieving a healthy balance between imposing structure and letting order emerge, we invite you to reflect on the following:

- How would you describe your ability to balance these two at this time? If a healthier balance is needed, what first step might you take toward that?
- What might you do to help others in your organization develop greater clarity about instability's role in creating stability?
- In your personal life, how does dynamic interaction influence you? How do you use disorder to form more order? Is there anything you

would do differently with a deeper understanding of how these two work together to create greater order?

- What examples can you think of in your organization where old order is replaced by new order? How does that happen now? What might you do to encourage more reordering?

SUMMARY

The fourth essential leadership practice for leading for improvement and innovation is let ideas collide. This practice reminds leaders that order emerges from a dynamic process of interaction and that it is ever changing, not static. In nature, systems and organisms continually reorder by using disorder to form greater order. At one time, science thought that disorder and order were dichotomous. Now, it is known that disorder supports the formation of greater order in nature's systems.

Natural systems reorder through a process where individual entities interpret the importance of a constant influx of new information and amplify that meaning through the system's networks. The information that strengthens and becomes the most important eventually engages the existing order. If it is significant, the system reorders to incorporate this information. This process is termed *dynamic interaction*.

Dynamic interaction plays a key part in how ideas become a part of the norm in society and in our lives. Organizations tend to adopt a view of order that is based in old science. This view perceives disorder as a threat to present order. Therefore, present order is protected. Newness causes perturbations, which may threaten present order, so organizations tend to carefully control and manage newness so that it can be incorporated into present order when necessary.

For school leaders, the importance of the leadership practice let ideas collide is that it honors that order is not static but dynamically adapting to changes in the environment. Rather than as something that needs to be imposed, the most meaningful reordering occurs from a meaning-making process. This means individual staff members need to make sense of new information and discuss that meaning with others across the system—changing the meaning and reinterpreting it. When ideas grow to where they cannot be ignored, it is important that current practice be challenged. The engagement of new ideas against existing practice means ideas are colliding. When these collisions lead to potent new ideas that can challenge old ways, reordering is possible. Leaders need to strengthen their skills at honoring this dynamic reordering process if we expect our educational systems to be adaptive and vital.

SBK High School: Letting Ideas Collide

As they have worked together, the leaders of SBK High School and its kindergarten through Grade 8 feeder district have made a conscious effort to create an environment where ideas can collide. They have created operating norms for their work sessions that reflect tolerance for ambiguities and messiness. Their interactions allow ideas to emerge from rich dialogue. From this, a natural composition has developed that balances structure with freedom. The leaders feel that their work has been exceedingly productive, and what they have learned about colliding ideas has now become part of their professional practice.

They are taking their ideas and process to a cross-section of people and providing them with information and opportunities to dialogue. Ideas are being debated and defended. A sign that the process is genuine is that the most authentic meaning of the needs of the 21st-century learner being generated come from their discussions weighed against their local experiences—rather than published material on the topic.

Conversations are taking place with each school board among various teacher, community, and parent groups. At times, the process seems messy and chaotic to the leaders, but they stay the course. They truly believe that order will emerge as groups engage with the ideas. Because there is no predetermined outcome, every idea is important.

It would be easier for the leaders in this district to just validate work that is being done at the state and national level and then impose this information on the staff. Instead, the leaders have fostered an opportunity to make meaning that is special and unique to the district. This will serve the students in innovative ways as they head into the future.

TEAM CONVERSATION STARTERS

Now, you have had the opportunity to develop knowledge about the four essential leadership practices: (1) *embrace dissonance*, (2) *create context*, (3) *change your field of perception*, and (4) *let ideas collide*. Take some time to engage one another in conversations about the following:

- When you think of these four practices together, what jumps out for you?
- Has your thinking changed since you began reading the book? If so, how?
- As a leader, what do you now see as possible within yourself that you did not see before?
- What do you now see as possible in your school, or setting, that you did not see as possible before?

Self-Assessment

Let Ideas Collide

You have reached the end of the presentation of the four essential leadership practices for creating systems that both improve and innovate. It is a good time to reflect on how your thinking has evolved from the start. Take some time to complete the self-assessment below—for the third and final time. After completing it, look back to your previous work. How does it compare? What has changed in your thinking? What does this mean for your leadership?

How do you prefer to create change in your work environment now?	Incrementally ♦——♦——♦——♦——♦——♦	In leaps
How do you as a leader react to disturbances to the status quo now?	Minimize them ♦——♦——♦——♦——♦——♦	Amplify them
What do you provide for your teams as they go about their work now?	Structure ♦——♦——♦——♦——♦——♦	Freedom
What kind of instruction do you now think will most improve student learning?	Standardized ♦——♦——♦——♦——♦——♦	Customized
What would most help people know what is important in your organization?	Directives ♦——♦——♦——♦——♦——♦	Relationships
How do you prefer information to move through your organization now?	Controlled ♦——♦——♦——♦——♦——♦	Free flowing
What type of problem solving do you now use when you analyze data?	Convergent ♦——♦——♦——♦——♦——♦	Divergent

Innovate the Way You Lead **10**

The principal goal of education is to create people who are capable of doing new things, not simply repeating what other generations have done—people who are creative, inventive discoverers.

—Jean Piaget, renowned
child psychologist and educator

The illiterate of the 21st century will not be those who cannot read and write, but those who cannot learn, unlearn, and relearn.

—Alvin Toffler, author and futurist

IN THIS CHAPTER

Everywhere you look the world is changing in response to an explosion of information. These changes are occurring in dramatic leaps, not at an incremental pace. Education has always been about preparing the next generation for the future they will inherit. If we are to meet that call today, we need a system of education that is responsive to changes in the external environment. For that to happen, we need leaders who foresee trends before they emerge and who are competent in creating systems that are able to respond quickly—systems that are capable of reordering while maintaining overall stability. These are new, profound challenges for educational leaders. Yet closing our eyes to the challenges will not make them go away.

To meet these challenges, a new repertoire of leadership practices is needed, a repertoire with new approaches to how systems are led. There is an old axiom that you cannot create something until you can imagine it. The intent of this book has been to create a new way for you to imagine what leadership is. Part II of the book has highlighted practices to help you do that. This chapter is intended to help you design actions to move your practice toward a new vision of leadership. It will address how to bring these images alive so that they can become part of your widespread practice.

Additionally, an action plan to develop momentum so that leadership practices on a broad level can tip in the direction of innovation will be provided. To accomplish this, you will be offered an opportunity for connecting with others so that your understandings can be amplified when your thoughts collide with those of others. Eventually, it is hoped that these collective understandings can challenge the status quo and create a new order for leadership. First, however, let's turn our attention to how to develop these practices in you.

THE JOURNEY STARTS WITH UNLEARNING

The quote by Alvin Toffler (1984) at the beginning of this chapter succinctly states an underlying message of the book: The imperative for leaders is to *learn, unlearn,* and *relearn.* In this quote, Toffler recognizes learning as a continuous cycle where letting go of old learning and replacing it with more relevant learning is a central element. These three stages place learning in the same context as reordering in natural systems where dissonance acts to break apart old order so that new order can form. Thinking of learning in this mind-set creates very different expectations than when one thinks of learning as something where new information is added to present knowledge. Central to this different expectation is unlearning: letting go of old constructs so that new, more relevant constructs can emerge. *Unlearning means that as one addresses new challenges he or she learns to let go of the way he or she has approached things in the past so that new ways have room to emerge.*

Dave Ulrich (2002) states the importance of unlearning in another way: "Innovation means letting go of old behaviors and policies and adapting new ones. Learning to forget becomes almost as difficult as learning to adapt" (p. 216). It is important for an innovation mind-set to learn to forget—to learn to unlearn—because there is no guarantee that what has worked in the past will work in the future.

The Future Is Not Necessarily Derived From the Past

Unlearning is important because the future can no longer be thought of as simply a derivative of the past. Think of what it means to enjoy musical recordings today . . . on your MP3 player, computer, or smartphone.

This technology could not have been predicted from the technology that produced vinyl LP recordings or CDs. To produce these new technologies, at some point, the formula for success in the recording industry needed to be unlearned so that new technology could emerge. If the industry was still trying to derive the next technology from LPs and CDs, you would not be downloading your favorite tunes to your personal devices.

Similarly, exactly what students will need in the future is not a simple derivative of the past. Look at our concept of classroom—a bedrock component of education for centuries. With the way that information is accessed and shared today, can anyone precisely predict what the classroom will look like or where learning will be taking place in 10 years? Educators at all levels need to recognize that success for tomorrow relies on unlearning some of the things we base practice on today. If this is not done, new initiatives will still be confined within the boundaries of current constructs. As leaders, we need to become more efficient

> As leaders, we need to become more efficient unlearners so that we can become better relearners.

unlearners so that we can become better relearners. To start with, we suggest that leaders begin to unlearn what it means to lead.

The Challenge Is Universal

In this book, we have presented the case that the hope for the future of our students is for schools to become not just better but different. This challenge is the same no matter the past levels of success or whether a school is public or private, urban or rural, small or large. Creating change that brings something new—something unimagined—in the present is the challenge. Its approach is universal despite the great differences in schools today. This type of change involves breaking apart present thinking to create the space for new ideas. This creates a different expectation for leaders than we have created in the past. Rather than reinforcing stability, the challenge for leaders today is about reordering, creating new thinking, seeing possibilities where in past they were not seen.

We have challenged you to think differently about the change elements of dissonance, identity, information, and order. Their true impact comes in what is created by their relationship to one another. In concert, they provide the attributes of a healthy, adaptive system. These attributes can greatly benefit organizations. These elements offer us a new way of thinking about people, work, and relationships—and about how leaders create the conditions for these to maximize potential.

For educators, these elements provide the possibility that, when present in the right combination, schools and districts have the ability to adapt to the changing world around them, increasing relevance, empowering individuals, and making education truly meaningful for all. To achieve these, as leaders, we all face the challenge to unlearn some of what we have learned about leading so that we can relearn practices better suited to the demands of the time in which we lead.

Innovate the Way You Lead

Unlearning involves the challenge of moving away from the traditional mind-sets of leadership—away from command and control—toward collaboration and connectedness. Hope for the system of education lies in moving toward leadership that creates context and sets people free within that context, toward leadership that encourages newness, which challenges existing thinking—leadership that allows new order to continuously emerge. This leadership balances improvement and innovation.

Throughout this book, we have highlighted the importance of innovating and how it differs from improving. We have explored those differences through examining the leadership practices needed to bring forth innovation balanced with improvement. Yet there is one last point we would like to emphasize. The most important innovation is not a new instructional method nor is it produced when a series of steps are followed. It is not about getting others to do more or be more. It is not a process that starts with an organizational initiative. Innovation starts within the leader. The most important innovation leaders can make is to innovate the way they lead.

> The most important innovation leaders can make is to innovate the way they lead.

Innovation, by its nature, is creating something that has not been thought of before—something that forms outside of predictable patterns. By encouraging you to innovate your leadership, we are encouraging you to develop an aspect of your leadership that you have not thought of before, one that is outside of your present patterns.

As we have been saying, innovation is about bringing forth something new. That simply cannot happen on an organizational level until it happens on a personal level—until the leader brings forth new perspectives in leading others.

Innovation can be a disruption; it can be unsettling to the status quo; there is risk involved; it is unpredictable; and it can be messy. These qualities are not valued in traditional organizations or within us personally. Yet to meet the challenges that our system of education faces, demands that we innovate. Embrace dissonance, create context, change your field of perception, and let ideas collide are practices that help us understand that we need not be afraid of the aforementioned elements—they are precursors to new order.

The power of these practices is found in how they change you. They are lights that illuminate the trail of an inner journey. The journey starts when new information generates dissonance within you, and that dissonance is referenced against a context of personal beliefs, values, and purpose. This collision of existing and new ideas sharpens, clarifies, and actualizes these beliefs into actions. These actions are based in new understanding—a new personal sense of order.

Observations About the Inner Journey

This inner journey is not a new phenomenon. It is ages old, written about in classic literature, contained in spiritual works of all ages, used in modern novels, a friend to screenwriters, and it is rediscovered by modern science. This journey is one of using disturbances to reorder, to move from a state of present capacity to one of higher capacity. It abundantly lies right before us, yet it is largely ignored in leadership theory.

Mystics on the spiritual path find that truth lies before them, where others do not see it. The secret to invention and entrepreneurship is seeing what others do not—opportunity where others see turbulence. A descriptive metaphor would be as if we are holding a diamond in our hand, yet we do not recognize it because it is covered in mud. Similarly, access to the inner journey lies hidden right before us.

Stepping onto the path of the journey is up to you. The Pilgrims set sail knowing that the future they faced was uncertain. What was certain was that to get to a better place they had to face new challenges and hardships. Creating a better life in the New

> Start the journey and the way begins to open up.

World did not promise to be easy. Yet they were willing to commit to the journey because to remain in their present state was unacceptable. It is also unacceptable for today's educational leaders. It is time to realize that the challenges today's schools face requires a departure from the thinking that created them. Incremental improvements will not allow us to keep pace with change. It is time to take the journey to new forms of leadership. Just as with leaving for the New World, this future holds potential, but its exact form is uncertain. The departure for the Pilgrims began with a belief that a better way of life could be created. The inner journey of leadership begins with a belief that a better educational future can be created.

The good news is we do not have to figure it out before departing. Start the journey and the way begins to open up. Do not wait for the expert to tell you how to innovate. We do not consider ourselves experts, but we have been on the journey. We have seen new potentials and are here to encourage others to begin the journey. The four leadership practices, (1) embrace dissonance, (2) create context, (3) change your field of perception, and (4) let ideas collide, help you see that there are other ways to lead. Now it is up to you. It was scary for the Pilgrims to leave the comfort of the known for the challenges of the unknown. However, when they saw the future through the current conditions and saw what was possible in another future, they knew they had to act. Ultimately, what we hope is that, after reading this book, you too will discover that you must act.

The most important thing we can leave you with is to encourage your inner journey—innovate the way you think about leadership and then act. Act on the possibilities that may be stirring within you to innovate the way you lead and work with others. There is no script, but consider how you spend your time. Is it in putting out fires, or is it in embracing dissonance? Is it in adhering to rules or helping others create new rules based on a clearly understood context? Is it in managing numbers or in amplifying ideas that may lead to breakthroughs? Is it in keeping a lid on things or letting ideas collide, creating a rich culture of possibility? Innovation is not a product or a process—it is the expectations you hold for yourself and for those you lead. The road to an innovative organization starts with changing the way you lead.

THE INNER JOURNEY

Let us lift the lid and look below the surface to see what happens when one takes an inner journey. Certainly, the result of an inner journey is a reordering of the individual. Just as with Campbell's (1991) hero journey, the inner journey involves a departure from a current state, followed by the development of new understanding that creates a new state of awareness, and finally, the return to acting on this new understanding by affecting one's outer actions. The path of the inner journey begins with an internal dialogue.

It may aid your ability to stimulate such an inner dialogue if you better understand part of the dynamic that unconsciously maintains the present state. Argyris and Schön (1978) studied organizations and found that it is common for there to be a difference between what they refer to as *espoused theories* and *theories in use.* Espoused theories are the views and values that people believe their behavior is based on. Theories in use are the views and values they use to take action.

Espoused Theories and Theories In Use

At first, this may appear to be a difference between what people in organizations say and what they do. However, Argyris, Putnam, and Smith (1985) articulate that the distinction is not between "theory and action but between two different 'theories of action'" (p. 82). In their studies, they conclude that what makes these different is that the values and beliefs that form the two theories are fundamentally different. They believe that a person's theories in use are derived from beliefs about the need for unilateral control of the environment and task and unilateral protection of self and others. In contrast, they find that espoused theories are derived from values that are consistent with more altruistic concepts such as sharing control, participation in design and implementation of action, and a high degree of freedom of choice. Furthermore, they suggest that people are unaware that their theories in use are often not the same as their espoused theories.

The point Argyris, Putnam, and Smith (1985) make is that people genuinely do not notice the differences between these two because subconsciously the reality of their theories in use are distorted to bring them in alignment with their espoused theories. For example, when creating visions and missions, or when planning for future improvements, leaders may genuinely believe in the values that are developed in this process—wide participation, unifying values, and effective solutions to problems. These constitute the espoused theories. On a daily basis, however, leaders operate from a second set of beliefs: their theories in use, which are generally based in strategies for control and protection. So in planning, they authentically value the importance of involving others in decisions. Yet when it is time for implementing planning decisions, they may believe that by telling people the thinking behind the plan and answering their questions before mandating the action that they are involving people in the process. The perception of their theories in use has been unconsciously distorted to bring them in line with their espoused theories.

The point we are making is that it can aid an inner journey to make one's espoused theories and theories in use more visible so that the gaps between them can be examined. The challenge for educational leaders is to engage in reflection that attempts to enlighten these differences and close the gap between them. The gap between espoused theories and theories in use provides a great opportunity to fuel the inner journey that breaks apart current practice and creates the opportunity for the emergence of new practice.

We have seen leaders speak articulately about the need for things such as out-of-the-box thinking only to find that when the opportunity to really bring it to life presents itself, it is unknowingly dampened, leaving the leader to later wonder why no one is coming up with out-of-the-box ideas. For instance, at a meeting a principal may suggest that he or she would like to have each of the teachers use a new technology that could really enhance instruction only to have the idea dampened by the superintendent because it would make this principal's school too different from the others. Or after being encouraged by a principal to do what's right for kids, a teacher suggests a way to change the lunch schedule to better accommodate learning only to have it shot down by the principal because it would take too much to redo the schedule already drafted.

We want to emphasize that these are not bad people and such occurrences are common. The gap between espoused theories and theories in use is in all of us, working all the time. What we are saying is that if you want to help your organization become better at balancing improvement and innovation, the place to start is to begin by holding courageous conversations that explore the gap between these two theories as it relates to the four leadership practices. The result of such activity is to shift your sense of what you expect from yourself and what to expect from others. This is how one begins to innovate the way he or she leads. The door is open. Are you ready to step through it?

Planning Your Inner Journey

At this time, we would like to offer you a tool for structuring your inner journey. The intent of this tool is to create an inner dialogue that is rich—where your thoughts can collide with your hopes, your dreams, and your present reality. Colliding new understanding can trigger new leadership actions that innovate the way you lead. Just as with the other activities in this book, the significance of what comes from the process of using this tool depends on how open you are to a frank inner dialogue. The path of the inner journey we are offering you is represented in Figure 10.1.

This diagram represents a process you can use to start the journey to innovating your leadership. At the heart of this process is a well-established planning tool to examine where one wants to be, where one is at presently, and then develops strategies to close the gap. A creative tension is produced between where one wants to be and where one is at presently. This leads to the generation of possible actions that can eventually move you and/or your organization to achieve the desired state. To

Figure 10.1 Structuring Your Inner Journey

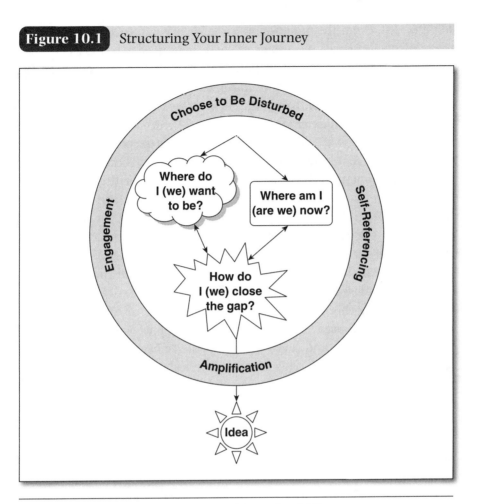

complete the process, a new twist has been added. Use this triad of perspectives to become more aware of the interplay of the innovative attributes within your thinking. The idea is that as you become more aware of how these attributes work within your field of thought, you can begin to establish them as a mind-set for leading others.

Use this process to develop insights into a part of your leadership practice that needs to be unlearned and to uncover where relearning can take place. It is important to go through this action-planning step internally—start by getting to know yourself in a deeper way than you have in the past. After you become comfortable with this internal process, it can be taught to and used with your students, staff, or team.

The point is to internalize the attributes of innovation and use them in a continuous cycle: Choose to be disturbed by something affecting your organization, and then reference that disturbance against your organization's sense of self. From this interaction, new ideas begin to spark, and their meaning needs to become amplified. These ideas need to be looked at from many perspectives so that their meaning can change and grow stronger. If the emerging idea grows and matures, it then needs to engage other ideas on a broader level, competing against or complementing them so that a new order can emerge.

The cycle of the attributes of innovation helps to create turbulence so that ideas can collide with deep thoughts, desires, visions, and current reality until something new sparks. This spark is an idea that was not present before; it is a leap in a new direction. It is not someone else's idea fit to your situation. It is new. It is one of those things that you know when you "see" it—when it takes form out of the chaos of unlearning, reflection, and self-examination. It is unproven, but it is something that intuition tells you will make a difference. This is the idea that suddenly all the turbulence coalesces around; it is the clearing of the fog. When it comes, it is time to take this idea out from your inner dialogue and share it with others. You have used the inner journey to depart your present state, become enlightened, and develop a new capacity. Now, it is time for you to get feedback from others. This process cycle is shown in Figure 10.2.

This does not mean that your idea is fully formed or that it is in a state that is ready to be implemented. It is in a state that allows you to engage others in your new understanding. The idea may need to go through a similar cycle with others in your organization. This is time to think about the leadership practices we have presented and the tips for bringing them to life. It is time to think how you can use these practices to bring emerging ideas to others to consider in relationship to current situations and problems. This interaction will alter and change the meaning of your idea to some extent—and this is good. This strengthens the idea and gets it ready for wide-scale use.

During this process of engaging others and having its meaning changed, you may need to loop the altered idea back into the process of internal dialogue where it moves through the cycle of testing it against your vision of where you want to be, where you are now, and how to get there. This internal to external thought flow will become something that you use fluidly and regularly. Over time, it should become second nature to you as part of a new leadership tool. As with all things, one needs practice before it becomes second nature. To that end, we have developed questions to guide you through the steps.

By now, you should be familiar with this inner reflection through the courageous conversation exercises we have been providing. Think of this as a new, but deeper, courageous conversation. Use this process to develop a plan of action that can lead you to leadership innovations. One word of caution, do not think of this as a linear process. Remember, it is important

Figure 10.2 Innovate the Way You Lead

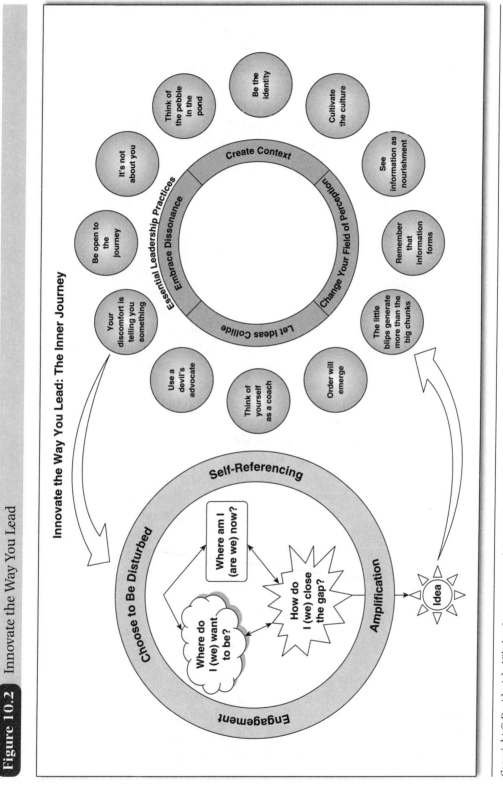

Innovate the Way You Lead: The Inner Journey

Essential Leadership Practices

Create Context

Embrace Dissonance

Change Your Field of Perception

Let Ideas Collide

- Think of the pebble in the pond
- Be the identity
- Cultivate the culture
- See information as nourishment
- Remember that information forms
- The little blips generate more than the big chunks
- Order will emerge
- Think of yourself as a coach
- Use a devil's advocate
- Your discomfort is telling you something
- Be open to the journey
- It's not about you

Self-Referencing

Choose to Be Disturbed

Engagement

Amplification

Where am I (are we) now?

Where do I (we) want to be?

How do I (we) close the gap?

Idea

to create an inner dialogue where ideas can spark and collide. The leadership innovation you are searching for comes unexpectedly—it cannot be predicted or foreshadowed—it is a leap to somewhere new, not a series of incremental steps. So let your thinking bounce around between these stages. Find ways to make your thinking visible: draw diagrams, write reflectively, jot down notes, and capture your dreams. They are all part of creating the conditions where you can innovate your leadership.

ACTION PLAN FOR INNOVATING THE WAY YOU LEAD

Getting Ready

Let's get started. We recommend you keep a reflective journal as your companion while you work through this action plan. Keep this accessible so that as thoughts surface throughout the day you can capture them. We also recommend you find a little time at the beginning or end of your day when you discipline yourself to take a few quiet, reflective moments to dedicate to this planning. Once you have a way to keep track of your thoughts, start to jot down notes, create images, capture key phrases, or important questions that come to mind as you go through the action-planning steps. Let these thoughts percolate and simmer in the back of your mind throughout the day. Later, as thoughts, ideas, and/or questions emerge, record them, and go on to other things. Make your reflective journal the garden for your growing wisdom.

Remember that all throughout this inner journey, the attributes of innovation should be in play; let your thinking be disturbed; constantly, reference this against your self-identity; let thoughts amplify, diminish, and bump up against other images; and let these emerging thoughts engage your mental models. As you work through the steps, some of the things you notice may start to make you feel uncomfortable. Don't rework them to ease your discomfort; move into that discomfort slowly. These are the nuggets for you to refine into gold.

Action Plan Step 1: Where Do I Want to Be?

This step is about identifying your preferred future (see Figure 10.3). This is not a head exercise—this is a whole-being exercise. A preferred future is based on the premise that if we envision something clearly from the deepest part of our being—our emotions, our desires, our hearts, our whole self—our life begins to move toward that mock-up. When you go deep within your being, where do you want your leadership to take your organization? By this we mean, where do you and your organization want to be at some point in the future (1 year, 5 years, 10 years, or more)?

Figure 10.3 Innovate the Way You Lead: Where Do I Want to Be?

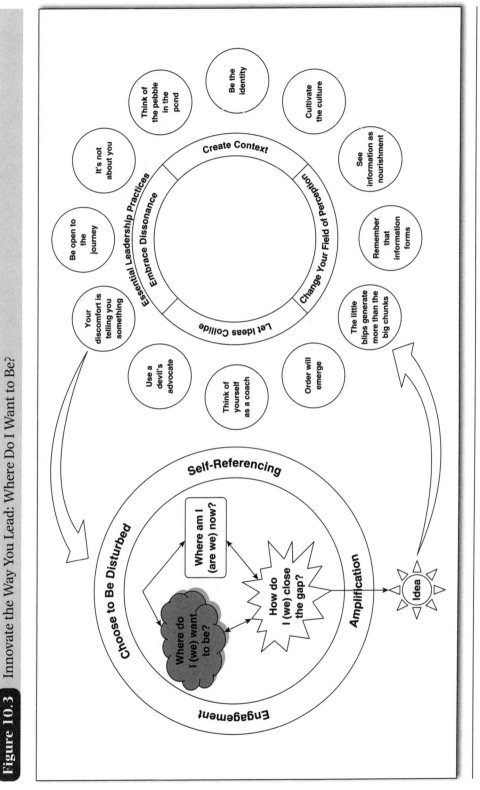

This process is like peeling back the layers of an onion. There is more under the surface than what first will appear. Make sure to give yourself the space and patience to get to a deeply seated, passionate vision. To that end, let your thoughts bond into important ideas. Play with the key elements of your emerging vision—let them come and go lightly through your thoughts; do not squeeze them too hard or demand complete form from them at this time. Most of all, do not act on them yet. This is a time to dream of possibilities; acting too early or sharing them with others too soon could crush them.

However, it may be beneficial to put out "test balloons" to others. Ask questions about how they envision the future, or ask what-if questions. It is important to write about what you are envisioning and use key phrases as filters as you watch and listen to others around you. Spend time gradually solidifying these thoughts until you begin to identify with this future in your heart and in your mind. Consider the following in your reflective journal. Then fill in your thoughts and/or sketches in the cloud-shaped space:

- Envision a school organization that is really meeting the challenges of preparing students for the future. What are students saying and doing? What is the staff saying and doing? Be specific: How are they reacting to dissonance? How are they using your organization's identity? How are they responding to information? How are they creating order and reordering?
- What are the three most important things that your organization stands for in this envisioned future?
- How does your organization measure success in this envisioned future?
- A national news organization wants to feature your school, district, or university as a benchmark of what is possible. What does their report highlight?

Figure 10.4 Innovate the Way You Lead: Where Am I Now?

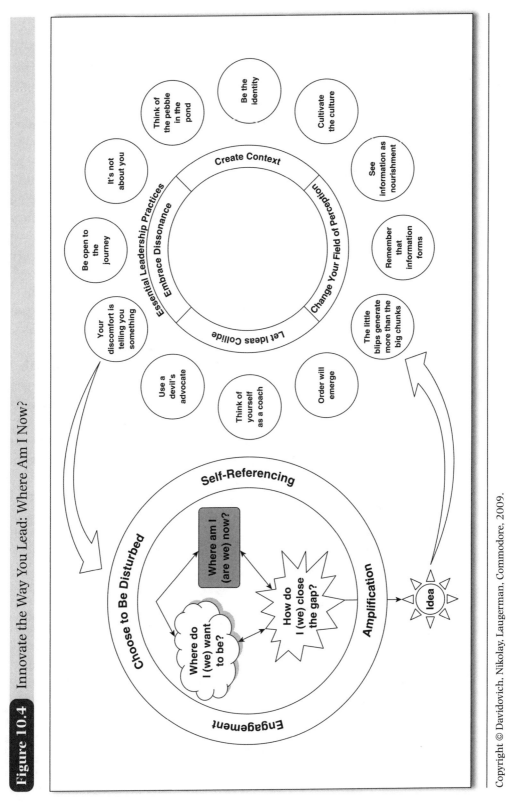

Action Plan Step 2: Where Am I Now?

In this step, it is time to consider where you (and/or your organization) are now (see Figure 10.4). Keep your reflective journal accessible. In particular, this stage will help you identify what your (and/or your organization's) practices, beliefs, and visions say about expectations for students and the future they are headed for. During this step, think about the present state that is created from the interaction between the espoused theories and the theories in use. The first part of this is to consider your espoused theories. As you did previously, let these ideas develop in layers. Observe your communications from a broader perspective by reflecting about what you are hoping that your communications (formal and informal, verbal and nonverbal) say to others about the beliefs, ideas, and theories that you espouse.

The second step is to shift to examining the theories in use. These are harder to identify because of the filters we subconsciously put in place to align them to our espoused theories. For insight, watch how others respond to what you say and do. During this step, it is very helpful if you can gain a detached perspective—a view from a higher perspective, as if looking down on your situation from a hilltop.

Next, the focus becomes making the difference between espoused theories and theories in use more visible. Then, evaluate the effect the gap between them has on the current state of your organization and your leadership. Give yourself time to record your thoughts and observations about the current state of your organization, its leadership, and your leadership. Be as frank and honest as possible in your observations—and also, be as kind as possible to yourself and others.

Remember that any gaps between these two types of theories stems from using two different theories, not from being disingenuous. What you are creating is a snapshot of where you and your organization are now. Just as with a photograph in the darkroom, take the time to let it develop. Let the chemicals for the developing snapshot be the four attributes of innovation.

Consider the following in your reflective journal. Then fill in your thoughts and/or sketches in the rectangle:

It is time to consider your espoused theories. Think back to recent conversations and communications you have had. What beliefs/ideas/theories have you been trying to communicate to others about student learning? What does this say about what you are advocating for to prepare students for the future?

- What do leaders in your organization say is important? What theories and beliefs are at the root of what they are saying?
- What buzzwords are prominent in your organization? What do these say about how your organization views its work to prepare students for the future?

- What three words or phrases capture your organizations espoused theories? What three words or phrases capture your espoused theories?
- Now consider your theories in use. What have your recent actions and decisions communicated to others about the beliefs and values your leadership is derived from? What theory would you say these actions and decisions are rooted in?
- What have your organization's recent actions and decisions communicated to others about the beliefs and values your leaders live? What theory is at the root of these?
- What kinds of responses do these actions and decisions produce in others? Why?
- What three words or phrases capture your organization's theories in use? What three words or phrases capture your theories in use?
- What does the information you have been generating in your reflections say about the gap between your theories in use and your espoused theories? Between your organization's theories in use and espoused theories? How does this influence your present state?

Action Plan Step 3: How Do I Close the Gap?

Considering where you want to be against where you are now probably reveals a gap (see Figure 10.5). This gap forms a creative tension for you to work with. Designing steps for closing the gap and moving toward your preferred future is the next step in your journey.

When it comes to designing action to move you closer to your plan, be careful not to "engineer" your plan right away. By this we mean, do not define the precise steps too early. The idea here is not to have the answers for a problem that you deliver to others who have yet to see the problems in the same way you do.

Figure 10.5 Innovate the Way You Lead: How Do I Close the Gap?

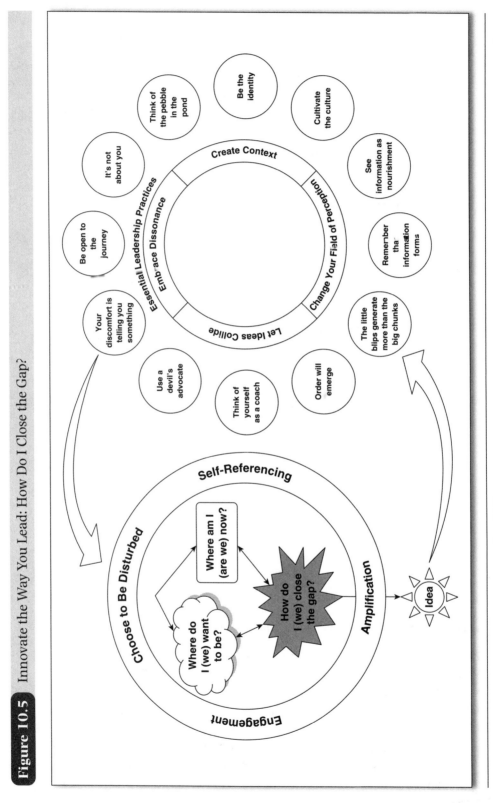

Remember that you are looking to innovate the way you lead—to develop an approach you are not presently using. Let the thoughts of where you want to be, where you are, and how to get there create a cauldron to mix ideas, hopes, and reality—all stirred by disturbance, self-referencing, amplifying, and engaging. Give time for these to interact with one another until something new forms. This is the essence of innovation—knowing it when you see it or feel it—when you don't own the idea, it owns you. After the idea begins to emerge, there will be time to articulate the details; don't force it too soon.

As you work through this step, record your thoughts in your journal. Identify big ideas that are starting to emerge that hold promise for innovating your organization and the way you lead. Plant those seeds in your thoughts for a few days, and observe what happens to them as they move from the background to the foreground of your thinking while you move through your day.

Consider the following in your reflective journal. Then fill in your thoughts and/or sketches in the star-shaped space:

- What do you not do now that if you did, it would allow you to achieve your desired state? What do others around you not do now that if they did, your organization's desired state could be achieved?
- What needs to be unlearned to help close the gap?
- What would have to happen for that to occur? What could you do to make it happen?
- How could closing that gap help achieve your vision? What relearning needs to happen to close that gap?
- What steps are you willing to take to make these changes?
- What specific idea emerges that will innovate the way you lead?
- How will you monitor and hold yourself accountable for these changes?
- Who can you connect with to help share your plan and help you monitor your progress?

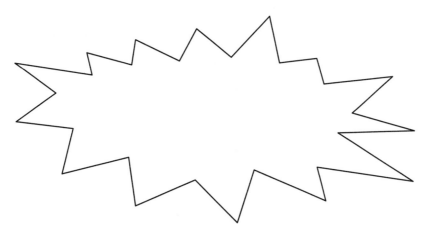

Action Plan Step 4: Bringing Your Idea to Life

Innovate the Way You Lead: Bring Your Idea to Life

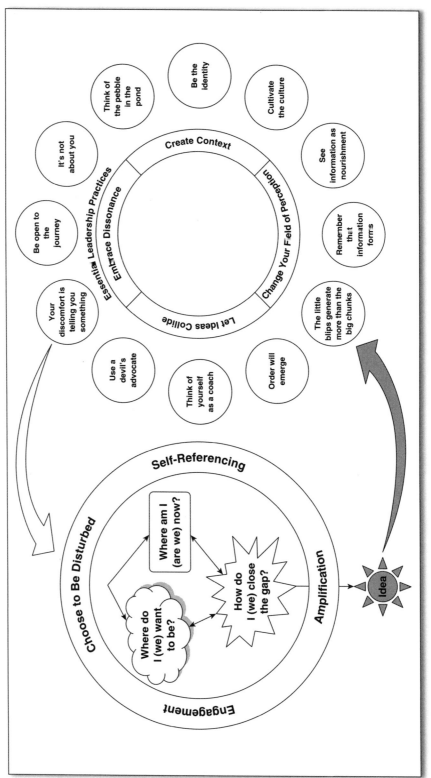

Helping Others Reorder Their Perceptions and Mental Models

By this point, you have reordered your perceptions and mental models about leading your organization. Hopefully, when you reach this stage, your thoughts and ideas about innovating your leadership will have strengthened to the point that you *must* act on them. This next step is about helping others reorder their perceptions and mental models as well. More than likely, realizing that sharing your ideas with others in ways that draws them into a new environment of engagement is part of your new understanding. In other words, by this point, we expect that you will know that telling people the answers you have developed is not the best approach. So this step of the process involves how to engage people in some of the same processes that produced your understanding as you share your ideas with them. This is where the four essential leadership practices come into play.

As others interact with your idea, it will change. This is exactly what you want. This process is not designed to have you become so attached to your idea that you do not let others play with it. The more others can bounce it around, the stronger it becomes. The intent is for your idea to seed the breaking apart of old thinking, to create new context and new information, and to encourage the collision of many ideas. This means that you may likely need to run the modified idea through the stages of the inner journey again. Doing so is done more quickly and efficiently the second or third time through. It is likely that this will become a constant filter for you as you process this and other ideas (see Figure 10.6).

Consider the following in your reflective journal. Then fill in your thoughts and/or sketches in the sun-shaped space:

- If you had only one minute to explain your new idea to someone, what would you say that captures the essence of your new understanding? What exactly, does innovating the way you lead mean for others?
- What dissonance will your ideas create in your organization? What can you do to frame this as a creative force, one that helps others embrace the dissonance your idea generates?
- How does your idea fit the current context of your organization? How can you elevate the current context so that your ideas are a logical extension of what is important to your organization?
- What can you do to engage others in generating amplifying information about the issues that surround your idea? How will you help others change their perceptions of using information as your idea moves the organization toward a preferred state?

- How will you create the conditions for others to interact with your idea in a way that lets ideas collide so that new order emerges?

SUMMARY

We hope that this signals a new approach to leadership for you—an approach where you feel empowered by the challenges you see and one where you empower your organization to address them as well. We also hope that you will continually look to enhance your leadership in ways that help both you and your organization innovate and improve.

Our children need educational leaders that possess the capacities you are developing. As a profession, we need to grow and spread the insights that you are uncovering. Imagine what is possible when the know-how of blending the diverse requirements of improvement and innovation into a coherent whole is amplified. Think of the potential generated when leaders talk to one another about what it means to do the following:

- Hold the system together while you help it break apart
- Preserve your organizational identity—yet be ready to help it evolve into something more
- Use information to inform and to form
- Use instability to strengthen stability

The future of our educational system needs your ideas to collide with other ideas. Today, ideas connecting across wide perspectives have the power to change the world. We ardently hope that voices sharing their insights into innovating learning and leadership can begin to build in profound ways. From this, a future of possibilities can become a reality. To that end, we encourage you to connect with others through the following Web site: www.beyondschoolimprovement.com.

Resource A

Glossary

Amplification is the process by which an idea gains strength and grows into something we may not have thought possible.

Amplifying feedback serves the function of compounding change in one direction with greater change in that direction.

Attributes of innovation are choosing to be disturbed, self-referencing, amplification, and engagement.

Bifurcation point occurs when a system, in its present structure, cannot deal with the meaning of agitation, so it either reorganizes to a higher level of complexity or disintegrates.

Change elements are dissonance, identity, information, and order.

Change field of perception means changing your perception with information and feedback, viewing information in relationship to forming new structures and amplifying meaning.

Choose to be disturbed means that you choose to be open to an experience despite how uncomfortable it makes you feel, trusting that it will result in something better.

Courageous conversations are inner dialogues that bring forth the courage and character necessary to move into disturbances to create the conditions for innovation. It is an internal dialogue that influences your spirit and your life.

Create context means to create a coherent, well-articulated, and deeply understood shared purpose where people know why they are there and are free to act within that purpose to better the organization.

Creating order is about generating structures that allows a system to maintain itself while also allowing it to adapt to changes so that it remains in sync with its environment.

Cultivating the culture means that you commit to creating connections between individuals and groups, in every way possible.

Dissonance is anything that causes fluctuation, perturbation, discomfort, or discord within the present state.

Disturbance happens when something disrupts the current state of a system—nudging accepted ideas to make us aware of their relationship to other ideas.

Dynamic interaction is the process where the individual entities that make up the system interact with a constant influx of newness.

Embracing dissonance means developing sensitivity to perturbations, to notice information that is discordant with your current state, to be an explorer.

Engagement happens when a new idea emerges and is allowed to engage with existing ideas to see what will develop along the way. It is the stage where the meaning of a new idea has grown in strength and must engage the current order.

Espoused theories are the views and values that people believe their behavior is based on.

Hero's journey has three parts:

> *Departure*—move out of your comfort zone
>
> *Fulfillment*—let colliding ideas and reflections lead to a place of inner peace and contentment
>
> *Return*—find a place to connect work and purpose

Identity is the shared intent that creates a system's sense of self. Our identity is our sense of self. It is the filter that makes sense of new information.

Improve means to enhance in value or quality: make better.

Improvement is about getting better within the current boundaries of a paradigm.

Information is the knowledge gathered by reading, listening, observing, and wondering about what one sees, thinks, and shares with others. It is any input that causes a system to respond and create meaning.

Innovate means to work outside of the current paradigm to make changes and to do something in a new way to achieve results unobtainable by improvement within the current structure.

Innovation is about doing things in a new way to achieve results unobtainable by improvement within the current systemic paradigm.

Innovation-oriented means to look for new ways of doing things to develop new capacities.

Leadership courage is the ability to let go of past practice, to move into uncertainty, to take adaptive action having minimal information, and to develop the trust that allows others to follow to the new destination.

Leadership practices include embrace dissonance, create context, change field of perception, and let ideas collide.

Let ideas collide is about creating the conditions for new responses to become the new norm—for the old ways to be replaced by new ways—recognizing reordering as something that emerges from supporting conditions rather than as an imposed will.

Lewin's change model identifies three steps: (1) unfreezing, (2) change, and (3) refreezing. The first step is the breakdown of meaning or relevance, followed by a change, and then the solidification of the new learning.

Mental model means the deep-thought patterns present in one's thinking that explains and defines the parameters of a construct.

Nanotechnology is the ability to manipulate matter at the molecular and atomic level.

Order is about replacing old ways with new ways without having everything fall apart.

Paradox is a statement or proposition that seems self-contradictory or absurd but, in reality, expresses a possible truth.

Regulatory feedback serves the function of keeping the system in balance, such as a thermostat.

S-curve is used to represent the growth and life cycles of systems and ideas from embryo development, to the spread of viruses, to professional careers, to technological advancements.

Self-organization is a process of attraction and repulsion in which the internal organization of a system, normally an open system, increases in complexity without being guided or managed by an outside source.

Self-referencing occurs when we reference a circumstance against a vision, mission, set of beliefs, or principles to guide our thinking and creative energies. Self-referencing means to reflect an idea against a vision, mission, set of beliefs, or principles.

Shared intent forms a system's identity and fosters an inspiring sense of purpose.

Strong identity occurs when people come to their profession believing they can make a difference with broad values, ideals, and beliefs.

System refers to interrelated, independent entities that form a complex, unified whole—both in nature and in social structures.

Theories in use are the views and values people use to take action.

Unlearning means that as one addresses new challenges, he or she learns to let go of the way he or she has approached things in the past so that new ways have room to emerge.

Resource B

Essential Leadership Actions

Resource C

*Continuum of Leadership
Behavior for Creating Change*

	Traditional organizational expectations	Moving away from tradition organization	Improvement mind-set	Moving toward self-organization	Innovation mind-set	Self-organizing organizational expectations
		Equilibrium			Disequilibrium	
Dissonance	**Don't want it!** Fluctuations are a threat. They need to be neutralized early so that the system does not go out of balance	Fluctuations distract us from what we are trying to accomplish, yet we have to show that we are responsive to change.	A little goes a long way—dissonance creates a need to get better at what we are doing.	Dissonance can be positive—we are trying to use it that way, but it still feels uncomfortable.	Dissonance creates opportunity—use it to create momentum for the leap to a new S-curve life cycle.	**Got to have it!** Dissonance creates the disequilibrium that keeps us on the innovative edge.
		Policy and Product			Sense-Making Process	
Identity	**Policy!** Identity is created through policy and procedures. They are what is needed to guide actions and behaviors.	A directive defined at the top creates identity. Groups implement new initiatives through this directive.	Identity is created by data: Initiatives involve producing a better product within that data range.	Identity is created by data: used to clarify purpose within mission/vision—action follows.	Self-referencing provides coherence that supports unique, localized solutions that create adaptive learning.	**Shared purpose!** A clear, coherent identity defines all activity. The system knows itself and everything filters through that.

	Traditional organizational expectations	Moving away from tradition organization	Improvement mind-set	Moving toward self-organization	Innovation mind-set	Self-organizing organizational expectations
Information	**Need to know basis!** The information the system pays attention to is generated at the top and improvement is regulated at the top.	Information analyzed at the top is passed down the organization to regulate and create improvement initiatives.	Sites use information to regulate student performance and create an improvement initiative.	Sites use information to understand a situation to develop new approaches.	Processes amplify information to form new mental models and design action for novel approaches.	**Free flowing!** Information the system notices can be generated from any point. Networks self-organize around that to amplify meaning and create novel responses.
	Controlled/Regulatory			Open/Amplified		
Order	**Control driven!** Newness is controlled and present order is protected.	Some newness creates interpretations of present order.	Newness is encouraged within current practice. Present order remains with some new approaches added.	Newness is allowed to create order outside of current practice. Some reordering begins.	Newness is allowed to challenge current practice so that reordering takes place.	**Emergent!** Newness is continually generated so that reordering is continuous.
	Predictability/Imposed			Interactive/Emergent		

References

Argyris, C., Putnam, R., & Smith, D. (1985). *Action science: Concepts, methods, and skills for research and intervention.* San Francisco: Jossey- Bass.

Argyris, C., & Schön, D. (1978). *Organizational learning: A theory of action perspective.* Reading, MA: Addison Wesley.

Black, P., & Wiliam, D. (1998, October). Inside the black box: Raising standards through classroom assessment. *Phi Delta Kappan, 80,* 139–148.

Blanchard, K. (2007). *The heart of a leader.* Colorado Springs, CO: David C. Cook.

Bridges, W. (1991). *Managing transitions: Making the most of change.* Reading, MA: Addison-Wesley.

Burke, J. (2002). When 1 + 1 = 3. In F. Hesselbein, M. Goldsmith, & I. Somerville (Eds.), *Leading for innovation and organizing for results* (pp. 185–196). San Francisco: Jossey- Bass.

Campbell, J., with Moyers, B. (1991). *The power of myth.* New York: Anchor Books.

Cheney, G., Ruzzi, B., & Muralidharan, K. (2005). *A profile of the Indian education system.* Retrieved January 25, 2008, from The National Center on Education and the Economy at http://www.skillscommission.org/staff.htm

Clarke, P. (2000). *Learning schools, learning systems.* London: Continuum.

Collins, J. (2005). *Good to great and the social sectors: Why business thinking is not the answer.* (Monograph). San Francisco: Elements Design Group.

Davis, I., & Stephenson, E. (2006, January). Ten trends to watch in 2006. *McKinsey Quarterly.* [Electronic version]. Retrieved December 17, 2008, from http://www.bmacewen.com/blog/pdf/McKinsey.2006.January.TenTrends.pdf

Donne, J. (1623). Devotions upon emergent occasions: Meditation XVII. Retrieved August 2, 2009, from http://www.ccel.org/ccel/donne/devotions.iv.iii.xvii.i.html

Friedman, T. (2005). *The world is flat: A brief history of the twenty-first century.* New York: Farrar, Straus, and Giroux.

Fullan, M. (2001). *Leading in a culture of change.* San Francisco: Jossey-Bass.

Fullan, M. (2008). *The six secrets of change.* San Francisco: John Wiley & Sons.

Goerner, S. (1999). *After the clockwork universe: The emerging science and culture of integral society.* Norwich, Great Britain: Floris Books.

Great Place to Work Institute. (2008). *Google: Take 2.* Retrieved November 17, 2008, from www.greatplacetowork.com/best/100best2008-google.php

Grossman, L. (2007). Time person of the year: You. *Time, 168*(26), 38–58.

Harigopal, K. (2001). *Management of organizational change: Leveraging transformation.* Thousand Oaks, CA: Sage.

Heifetz, R., & Linsky, M. (2002). *Leadership on the line: Staying alive through the dangers of leading.* Boston: Harvard Business Press.

Hesselbein, F., Goldsmith, M., & Somerville, I. (Eds.). (2002). *Leading for innovation and organizing for results.* San Francisco: Jossey-Bass.

Jobs, S. (2006). Retrieved December 3, 2008, from Thinkexist.com at www .thinkexist.com/quotations/innovation

Kahn, J. (2006, June). Welcome to the world of nanotechnology. *National Geographic, 209*(6), 98–119.

Kanter, R. M. (2002). Creating the culture for innovation. In F. Hesselbein, M. Goldsmith, & I. Somerville (Eds.), *Leading for innovation and organizing for results* (pp. 73–86). San Francisco: Jossey-Bass.

Kauffman, S. (1995). *At home in the universe· The search for laws of self-organization and complexity.* New York: Oxford University Press.

Kouzes, J., & Posner, B. (2009). To lead, create a shared vision. *Harvard Business Review, 87*(1), 20–21.

Lewin, R. (1999). *Complexity: Life at the edge of chaos* (2nd ed.). Chicago: The University of Chicago Press.

Marshall, S. (2006). *The power to transform: leadership that brings learning and schooling to life.* San Francisco: Jossey-Bass.

Marzano, R., Waters, T., & McNulty, B. (2005). *School leadership that works: from research to results.* Alexandria, VA: Association for Supervision and Curriculum Development.

Maxwell, J. (2003). *Attitude 101: What every leader needs to know.* Nashville, TN: Thomas Nelson.

Merriam-Webster's Online Dictionary. (2009). Retrieved January 8, 2009, from Merriam-Webster Online at www.meriam-webster.com/dictionary

National Center for Education Statistics. (2008).The Nation's Report Card—Mathematics report card. Retrieved January 12, 2009, from http://nces.ed.gov/nationsreport card/nde/viewresults.asp

National Center on Education and the Economy. (2007). *Tough choices or tough times: The report of the new commission on the skills of the American workforce.* San Francisco: Jossey-Bass.

National Nanotechnology Initiative. (2009a). *Education center.* Retrieved May 1, 2009, from http://www.nano.gov/html/edu/home_edu.html

National Nanotechnology Initiative. (2009b). *FAQs: Nanotechnology.* Retrieved May 1, 2009, from http://www.nano.gov/html/facts/faqs.html

O'Connor, K. (2009). *How to grade for learning, K–12* (3rd ed.).Thousand Oaks, CA: Corwin Press.

Partnership for 21st Century Skills, (2002). *Learning for the 21st century: A report and mile guide for 21st century skills.* Washington, DC.

Pascale, R., Millemann, M., & Gioja, L. (2000). *Surfing the edge of chaos: The laws of nature and the new laws of business.* New York: Crown Business.

Peters, T. (2005). *Leadership inspire, liberate, achieve.* London: DK.

Pink, D. (2005). *A whole new mind: moving from the information age to the conceptual age.* New York: Berkley.

Prensky, M. (2001, October). Digital natives digital immigrants. Retrieved October 23, 2008, from *On the Horizon* at http://www.marcprensky.com/writing

Prigogine, I., & Stengers, I. (1984). *Order out of chaos: Man's dialogue with nature.* Boulder, CO: Shambhala.

Reeves, D. (2001). *Making standards work: How to implement standards-based assessments in classroom, school, and district.* Denver, CO: Advanced Learning Centers.

Rogers, E. (1995). *Diffusion of innovations,* (4th ed.). New York: The Free Press.

Schein, E. (1999). *The corporate culture survival guide: Sense and nonsense about culture change.* San Francisco: Jossey-Bass.

Schein, E. (2007). *Kurt Lewin's change theory in the field and in the classroom: Notes toward a model of managed learning.* Retrieved February 13, 2008, from the Society of Organizational learning at http://www.solonline.org/res/wp/10006.html

Seely Brown, J. (1997). *Seeing differently: Insights on innovation.* Boston, MA: Harvard Business School Press.

Senge, P. (1990). *The fifth discipline: The art and practice of the learning organization.* New York: Doubleday.

Senge, P., Cambron-McCabe, N., Lucas, T., Smith, B., Dutton, J., & Kleiner, A. (2000). *Schools that learn: A fifth discipline fieldbook for educators, parents, and everyone who cares about education.* New York: Doubleday.

Senge, P., Scharmer, C., Jaworski, J., & Flowers, B. (2004). *Presence: Human purpose and the field of the future.* Cambridge, MA: The Society for Organizational Learning.

Singleton, G., & Linton, C. (2006). *Courageous conversations about race.* Thousand Oaks, CA: Corwin.

Spellings, M. (2008). Remarks at the Aspen Institute's National Education Summit: Washington, DC. Retrieved September 16, 2008, from http://www .ed.gov/print/news/speeches/2008/09/09152008.html

Stacey, R. (1992). *Managing the unknowable: Strategic boundaries between order and chaos in organizations.* San Francisco: Jossey Bass

Stiggins, R., Arter, J., Chappuis, J., & Chappuis, S. (2006). *Classroom assessment for student learning: Doing it right—Using it well.* Portland, OR: Educational Testing Services.

Stiggins, R. (2008, April). *A call for the development of balanced assessment systems.* (Assessment Manifesto). Portland, OR: ETS Assessment Training Institute.

Toffler, A. (1984). Science and change. In Prigogine, I. & Stengers, I., *Order out of chaos: Man's dialogue with nature* (xi–xxxi). Boulder, CO: Shambhala.

Tucker, R. (2008). Driving growth through innovation. San Francisco: Berrett-Koehler.

Ulrich. D. (2002). An innovation protocol. In F. Hesselbein, M. Goldsmith, & I. Somerville (Eds.), *Leading for innovation and organizing for results* (pp. 215–224). San Francisco: Jossey-Bass.

Wheatley, M. (1997, July). Goodbye, command and control. *Leader to Leader.* [Electronic version] Retrieved November 3, 2006, from http://www.margaret wheatley.com/articles/goodbyecommand.html

Wheatley, M. (1999a, September). Bringing schools back to life: Schools as living systems. In F. Duffy and J. Dale (2001), *Creating successful school systems: Voices from the university, the field, and the community.* Norwood, MA: Christopher-Gordon. [Electronic version] Retrieved November 12, 2006, from http://wwwmargaret wheatley.com/articles/lifetoschools.html

Wheatley, M. (1999b). *Leadership and the new science: Learning about organizations from an orderly universe* (2nd ed.). San Francisco: Berrett-Koehler.

Wheatley, M. (2005). *Finding our way: Leadership for an uncertain time.* San Francisco: Berrett-Koehler.

Wheatley, M. (2006). *The real world: Leadership lessons from disaster relief and terrorist networks.* Retrieved October 15, 2008, from Margaret J. Wheatley at http://www.margaretwheatley.com/articles/therealworld.html

Wheatley, M. (2007). Leadership of self-organizing networks: Lessons from the war on terror. *Performance Improvement Quarterly, 20*(2), 59–66. [Electronic version] Retrieved July 17, 2008, from http://www.margaretwheatley.com/articles/ Self-OrganizedNetworks.pdf

Wikipedia. (2008). *Ilya Prigogine.* Retrieved September 28, 2008, from http://en .wikipedia.org/wiki/Ilya_Prigogine

Wikipedia. (2009). *Self-organization.* Retrieved January 9, 2009, from http://en .wikipedia.org/wiki/Self-organization

Whitworth, L., Kimsey-House, H., & Sandhal, P. (1998). *Co-active coaching: New skills for coaching people toward success in work and life.* Mountain View, CA: Davies-Black.

Zohar, D. (1997). *Rewiring the corporate brain: Using the new science to rethink how we structure and lead organizations.* San Francisco: Berrett-Koehler.

Index